# BOUNDLESS:
# 2020
# the Anthology of the

# RIO GRANDE VALLEY INTERNATIONAL POETRY FESTIVAL

FlowerSong Press
McAllen, Texas 78501
Copyright © 2020 FlowerSong Press

ISBN: 978-1-7345617-9-1

Published by FlowerSong Press
in the United States of America.
www.flowersongpress.com

Set in Avenir

Typeset and design by Matthew Revert
www.matthewrevert.com

No part of this book may be reproduced without written permission from the publisher.

All inquiries and permission requests should be addressed to the Publisher.

# FLOWERSONG
PRESS

**Selected and Edited by
Edward Vidaurre**

Rio Grande Valley
International Poetry Festival
www.valleypoetryfest.org

Boundless is the official anthology of the Rio Grande Valley International Poetry Festival (VIPF), founded in 2008 by Daniel García Ordaz and Brenda Nettles Riojas. VIPF is held annually the last weekend in April in deep South Texas as a celebration of National Poetry Month.

for the essential worker, for the artist that creates when healing is necessary, for the youth searching for their place in this world, for those that left us, and for you… the reader

# Foreword

As I sit putting together these poems, I would have never thought: Is everyone on the table of contents going to be alive to see the print edition? Would I be here by the time it gets to the poets? Last year, when we got together to talk about the 13th Annual Valley International Poetry Festival I was excited to be named the Director of Operations. Especially when it came to putting together this anthology. With poems from all over the world coming in from Africa, Latin America, China, Europe, the Middle East and all over the U.S., I found one thing in common between us all: Our NOW is important for tomorrow. Who's tomorrow? It really isn't a for who? The poetry is a healing for the moment and for the ages.

This anthology is a split in section I and II, adult and youth writings. You will see the difference between the truth tellers (youth) and the healers (adults) who have lived a long truth of pain and experiences that have molded them into the writers they are today. Not saying that the adults don't tell the truth, but we seem to mask our truths and sometimes write the truth of others, whereas the youth poets are eager to tell their story front and center.

The truth right now is that none of us can hide our vulnerabilities and fears. Living and writing through a pandemic is something none of us have ever done. Many of the poems here are before the outbreak. The fear of a domestic terrorist, the pain of losing a mother, you'll find poems of resistance, and remembrance, children's poetry, ode to an avocado, and so much more...this collection is a sneak peak at what life was like before our normal was interrupted, but try explaining normal to a poet, I dare you.

Find that salve in the words of award winning poets, poets laureate, lifelong writers, novice writers, from all industries and work backgrounds, they come together to share their verses.

Thanks and gratitude to Daniel and Brenda for their friendship along with their families. May you all be blessed for another 13 festivals and much more.

From youth poet Natalie Viveros:

> "Love
> We all need it
> To survive,
> To live..."

I wish you all a long life, filled with love, healing touches, & quick recoveries from pain.

-Edward Vidaurre, Boundless Editor, Publisher FlowerSong Press

# Table of Contents

## Section One: The Healers

| | |
|---|---|
| 21 | Today's Gratitude Prayer: The Burning of the Sage |
| 23 | Inepo hamutta vichu (Yaqui: I am looking at the woman.) |
| 25 | Daily Affirmations |
| 27 | A Typical Saturday |
| 29 | Sundays |
| 31 | The Great Mystery |
| 33 | A Letter From Israel |
| 35 | Ransom Note Typed on an Old Underwood with an "O" That Won't Strike |
| 37 | You are the incense |
| 40 | My God |
| 41 | Seyewailo (Yaqui: Flower World) |
| 50 | Menstruation Hay(na)ku |
| 51 | Shades of Meaning |
| 53 | We Could Not Know |
| 55 | Como Hubiera |
| 60 | Remembering Mother |
| 62 | Way too Soon |
| 65 | Illuminado |
| 67 | Son |
| 68 | Pam |
| 70 | The Elevator at a Hispanic Serving University |
| 71 | Herencias Herreranáuticas |
| 74 | Weightless |
| 76 | Juan Romero and the Dead Kennedy |
| 81 | At the Fine Arts Gallery |
| 82 | Winter Road |
| 83 | Ausencia |
| 85 | Aberrant Thought While in a Check-out Line |
| 86 | LONG EL PASO AFTERMATH |

| | |
|---|---|
| 87 | I Remember the Alamo (Differently) |
| 93 | Claudia Patricia Gomez Gonzalez Is Returned To Mother Earth |
| 95 | Issues of: |
| 98 | América para los americanos: Central America, 2016 |
| 100 | Perilous Borders |
| 102 | When I Wear Bob Kaufman's Eyes |
| 103 | Brother Shaman |
| 105 | Alone Together |
| 107 | Urethral Rocket |
| 108 | Despair |
| 110 | Homeless Man |
| 111 | Homelessness |
| 113 | MY BODY AS A BACKPACK FOR LOVED ONES & THINGS THAT SIT ON A WHEELCHAIR |
| 115 | Solitude |
| 117 | TAPS |
| 119 | This Poem Doesn't Exist |
| 121 | Books, Balls, and Candy |
| 123 | Nursery of Winds |
| 125 | Through the Year |
| 126 | Foreign Service |
| 128 | Books |
| 130 | The Awkward Book |
| 131 | Campground |
| 132 | If you are like me |
| 134 | Class Consciousness |
| 136 | 1 is 2nd |
| 138 | 45 |
| 140 | Drive Down 77 |
| 142 | Expiation |
| 143 | Samaria |
| 145 | Samaria |
| 147 | Tragedy and Comedy |
| 148 | 3 Haiku- A Happy Young Guy/Unknown/Close my Eyes |
| 149 | Johnny |

| | |
|---|---|
| 152 | The Cost |
| 157 | The Flight to Johannesburg |
| 159 | Main Street |
| 161 | Math |
| 162 | Amazon |
| 164 | Budding Romeo, Ghazal (a poetry form in Hindi & Urdu) |
| 166 | Ave de día |
| 168 | This is all he knows |
| 169 | Awaiting the Heart Attack |
| 170 | Worn |
| 172 | I Write to Extract |
| 174 | Beatitudes for the Hideous |
| 175 | El peligro de la noche violada |
| 177 | Country Nights |
| 179 | The Winter |
| 180 | Desert Lament |
| 181 | The Great American Windmill Bob Kaufman Destroyed |
| 182 | A Little Less Sad |
| 184 | Isabel |
| 186 | Academic Award For the Movie, "Ars Poetica" |
| 187 | Claremont Avenue |
| 189 | Traficante |
| 193 | Ode to an Avocado |
| 195 | Bowie's Lazarus |
| 197 | Chorizaso |
| 198 | Release It |
| 200 | Abused in the rain |
| 201 | Niña sin nombre |
| 204 | Girl with no name |
| 207 | The WIllows |
| 209 | December 3rd, 2007 |
| 211 | Thirty Something |
| 213 | The lost leaf |
| 215 | I am not ashamed |
| 216 | Before Work |
| 218 | Wick Work |
| 220 | A Purple Cow/A Tabby Cat/A Yellow Rat |

| | |
|---|---|
| 222 | Losing Sight |
| 224 | 9 |
| 225 | 9 |
| 227 | The revolving doors |
| 229 | Shipley Do-nuts |
| 231 | The Earth |
| 232 | LAUGH, DREAM |
| 234 | Mountain time |
| 235 | A query |
| 236 | ay, Padre Viento |
| 238 | Children have left the house |

## Section Two: The Truth-Tellers

| | |
|---|---|
| 241 | Half and Half |
| 243 | Undying Love |
| 244 | Fractured and Twisted |
| 246 | Happiness |
| 247 | Abuelo |
| 248 | Adolescencia |
| 249 | Rainy Days |
| 250 | Abuela |
| 252 | Una estrella para mí |
| 253 | Stars |
| 255 | Letter to My Parents |
| 257 | Media Naranja |
| 259 | Border Town Tongue |
| 260 | Dear Anonymous |
| 261 | Anónimo |
| 262 | My sunflower |
| 263 | Wasn't her |
| 264 | Dear Dad, |
| 265 | Te vi de nuevo |
| 267 | I saw you again |
| 269 | Tiempo |
| 270 | La vida del portero |
| 272 | Crash |

| | |
|---|---|
| 274 | The Bus Stop |
| 275 | Alone |
| 276 | Mi gran amigo |
| 277 | Ya no siento nada por tí |
| 279 | Nature |
| 280 | Sí, Hispano |
| 282 | Yes, Hispanic |
| 284 | I wait |
| 285 | El Rancho |
| 287 | The Ranch |
| 289 | Para Siempre |
| 291 | Potholes |
| 293 | Los mas feos |
| 295 | You |
| 296 | Mi Abuela |
| 297 | My Grandma |
| 298 | Amor Verdadero |
| 299 | First Love |
| 301 | Primer Amor |
| 303 | Mi Mayor Bendición |
| 305 | Recuerdos |
| 307 | Memories |
| 309 | Tu forma de ser |
| 310 | The way you are |
| 311 | Oh! My Love |
| 312 | Oh! Mi Amor |
| 313 | Veterans |
| 315 | Monstrous |
| 317 | Atrapada |
| 319 | A Love Story |
| 321 | The Botany of Dreams |
| 323 | Extraño |
| 324 | Innocencia |
| 325 | Dad |
| 326 | Padre |
| 327 | Blank |
| 329 | Blanco |

| | |
|---|---|
| 331 | El caballo de mis sueños |
| 332 | The horse of my dreams |
| 333 | Dilemas |
| 334 | Hermanito |
| 335 | Cosmetics ≠ Society |
| 337 | El Amor es Hermoso |
| 339 | Love is Beautiful |
| 341 | Anger |
| 343 | Una vez más |
| 344 | One more time |
| 345 | Felicidad |
| 346 | Happiness |
| 347 | Creciendo |
| 348 | Dam |
| 350 | Hourglasses Tick |
| 352 | If you gave a person immortality and a myriad of things, what would they do? |
| 354 | Fue un error |
| 356 | It was a mistake |
| 358 | Fácil |

# Dedication

## To our families

**In honor of:**
Jan Seale, 2012 Texas State Poet Laureate, McAllen, Texas
Emmy Pérez, 2020 Texas Poet Laureate, McAllen, Texas
Rodney Gomez, 2020-2021 City of McAllen Poet Laureate

**In memoriam:**

Dr. Gloria E. Anzaldúa
Jovita González
Dr. Américo Paredes
Dr. Harold Rodinsky
Rául R. Salinas
Arturo Saldaña
Trinidad Sánchez, Jr.
Xavier Hinojosa
Hawk Galván
Roberto de la Torre

# ONE

## The healers

# Today's Gratitude Prayer: The Burning of the Sage

"Beware the Ides of March!"
~ to Caesar (not that one)

Thank you Spirit for my survival
For the Survival of those that I love
For the survival of All
May we grow old and strong together
May we rededicate ourselves to you
May we work for the good of The Earth
For the good of All

(facing The Four Directions, turning, reaching up and offering Sage)

TIAHUÍ! (to the Spirits of The East!)
TIAHUÍ! (to the Spirits of The South!)
TIAHUÍ! (to the Spirits of the West!)
TIAHUÍ! (to the Spirits of North!)

Great Spirit, thank you for The Earth
Thank you for Water, may we protect Her
Thank you for the air that we breathe
May we keep it clean
Thank you for The Earth that I walk upon
May you keep me strong and able to walk on

May you continue to protect me
So that I continue to work for you
For The Earth, and Protector of Water
For the benefit of ALL.

(and bring me one who loves me
a nice guy who'll take me camping.)

-*Lorna Dee Cervantes*

Born in San Francisco, raised in San José, Barrio Horseshoe, Lorna Dee Cervantes was a self-taught activist by 15, an instant mother at 19, taught herself how to run her own printing press and was Founding Editor/Publisher of MANGO Publications at 20, and the author of EMPLUMADA at 24. A XícanIndX poet (Chumash/Purépecha), Cervantes (PhD, History of Consciousness) was a Professor of English for 20 years at CU Boulder, serving as Director of Creative Writing. She identifies as Indigenous American with 5 books in print and writing 5 more in Seattle

# Inepo hamutta vichu
(Yaqui: I am looking at the woman.)

If the rumble of the remote
tree disturbs you
it is not for lack of concern.

It is the Tosai Bwia "white earth"
calling for the disconcerted distress
of the unjust realm spread across
the bucolic sagebrush.

It is the concern of the collective spirit;
the unsettled concern of the mother up late
pending on the arrival of her son who sneaks
through the slits, walls, and vents.

If the remorse of the unjust world
leaks through the withered eyes
of the grandfathers
it because it has been felt
at the marrow of the bone
ached at bitter coldness;
distressed at the abandonment.

If the woman hears the rumbling
from the trunk as a man
it is because she can not help

but alleviate the bundle of
convoluted agony that staggers
through the empty halls and
vacuous  home.

The scent of the man that
pervades the forgone empty
curtains of the house is more
in the mind and the nostril
than anywhere.

If we are looking at the woman
it is because we hope for an understanding
of the future; the unspeakable; the gentle murmur
of her jet black hair; her supple hands
and her ability to translate.

-*Tezozomoc*

Tezozomoc is a Los Angeles Chicano Poet and 2009 Oscar Nominated Activist and has been published by Floricanto Press, "Gashes!: Poems and Pain from the halls of injustice", a collection of poetry, ISBN-13: 978-1951088040, 9/2019. He has also been published in the following journals: The Oddball Magazine, 06/19/2019. Spitpoetzine, Volume 6, 6/15/2019. The Silver Stork, silverstorkmagazine.weebly.com/, 2018.

# Daily Affirmations

I'm lucky to be in the United States.
I'm lucky to be working.
I'm lucky to have friends.
    *Do not think about the family I left 7,000 miles away.*
I'm lucky to know English.
I'm lucky to drive.
I'm lucky to have a partner.
    *Do not think about the 5 years I've been waiting.*
I'm lucky to have come on a plane.
I'm lucky to have a roof & this bread.
I'm lucky to ask for mercy.
    *Do not think about how I'm still waiting.*
I'm lucky to not notice the slurs.
I'm lucky to drink clear water.
I'm lucky to not be alone.
    *Do not think about the time I spent in a cell.*
    *Do not think about the scars across*
    *my face, my arms, my body.*
    *Do not think about what might*
    *happen if I go back home.*
I'm lucky to be breathing.
I'm lucky to be speaking.
I'm lucky to be living.

People tell me I'm lucky,
so I must be lucky. I guess I must forget

my breath is in the hands of laws that do not want me.
I must forget the nights when I cannot sleep.
I must forget that I might forget
my childhood only to be sent
back to the nightmares I've lived.
I guess I must forget
how this country looks at an immigrant.

>*Do not think about my status*
>*& remember to have a good day.*

-Tatiana Figueroa Ramirez

Tatiana graduated with a B.A. in English Literature and a minor in American Studies from the University of Maryland, Baltimore County (UMBC). She is a VONA/Voices Alumna having studied under award-winning poets Willie Perdomo and Danez Smith. Tatiana has been published in Queen Mob's Teahouse, The Acentos Review, A Gypsy's Library, and Here Comes Everyone among other publications. She currently performs, facilitates workshops, and hosts events in the greater Washington D.C. area, having previously done so in New York, Miami, Philadelphia, Puerto Rico, and the Dominican Republic, including venues such as New York University, The Kennedy Center, and The Howard Theatre. Tatiana is the author of COCONUT CURLS Y CAFÉ CON LECHE and Despojo (FlowerSong Press, 2020).

# A Typical Saturday
*In Memory of Edwin, Joseph, Kameron, Leilah, Mary, Raul, and Rodolfo.

ISun scorches the West Texas desert.
Air conditioners hum on high.
At a local pool, sun-drenched arms
rest on cobalt noodles, feet splashing.
Teenagers take selfies wherever they are.
Some guy runs a stop sign and is pulled over.

He steps out of his car and shoots
a Texas Highway Patrolman just like that.
Steps back in his Honda, his AR-15
beside him, and speeds down I-20.
Everybody's a moving target, turning
Odessa into a freakish firing range.

Twelve hundred miles away I comb through
comforters at the Assistance League Thrift Store,
looking for something splashy, Rothko red & yellow
to brighten my bed. Nothing found except a book,
*Hillbilly Elegy*
I read outside as my friend
searches through cotton shorts and shirts.

70 degrees, breeze off the Pacific. Normal
Santa Barbara weather except when wildfires

burn the Sycamore & Laurel, and ash suffocates us all.
But today doesn't start like one of those days.
With a soft ping, a news alert appears on my phone:
*Eight people killed in a shooting spree in Odessa, Texas.*

For you it was your last afternoon.
You were at the car dealership with your family.
You were standing in your parents' front yard.
You were waiting at a traffic light with your wife and two children.
You were talking on the cell to your sister.
You were driving home from work.

You were a veteran of Afghanistan.
You were from El Paso.
A random shot took your lives.
The eighth dead held the gun.
The temperature rose to 96.

-chella courington

Chella Courington is a writer and teacher whose poems and stories appear in numerous anthologies and journals including Spillway, The Collagist, and The Los Angeles Review. Her novella, Adele and Tom: The Portrait of a Marriage, is forthcoming from Breaking Rules Publishing. Originally from the Appalachian South, Courington lives in California with another writer.

# Sundays

Sundays are supposed to be like warm naps under the window.

Sundays are supposed to be like the sweet ice cream dripping in-between your fingers.

Sundays are for barbeques.
They smell like a pot of boiling beans with bacon. They smell like Fabuloso.
They sound like the slow-cooked sizzle of barbacoa.
Like bibles and smiles.

But for you Sunday was cruel whipping wind that ripped the ribbon out of your hair.
Sundays smelt like rust.
Domingos smelt like cologne that choked.
Domingos felt like forced smiles and itchy sweaters.
Domingos looked like the tattered page of Luke 6:22.
Domingos sounded like the springs of a squeaky trampoline.

This Domingo was just like the last Domingo.

Domingo made you lie down on a rusty trampoline.
It trapped you when the familia was asleep waiting on Monday.
It placed its heavy hands on your thigh and said – *shhh!*

Domingos like this one should be scratched out of our family's

calendar.
It should have thick black scribbles on its square.

But papa and mama and tia and abuela tell you – *No! Don't do that!*
*That's your tio's birthday!*

And they don't know about Domingo.
They don't know about Sunday.
They don't know that this Domingo,
was just like the last Domingo.

*-Lea Colchado*

Lea Christine Colchado is a lover of words and stories, especially from Chicanas. She currently is a Rhetoric and Composition graduate student at Texas State University where she explores and plays with the power of words, language, and identity.

# The Great Mystery

Pre-dawn cognition fumbles about
  in shades of fuzzy grey ---
  nothing to grasp
  nothing too real.
What wakes the eye on a morning like
  this is a mystery.

Nature wraps these hills
  in the vapor of her still breath ---
  white and thick she lies,
  blurring lines of symmetry,
  protecting her own.
Ethereal dreams of fulfillment
  soaring through their minds,
  soporific birds like philosophers
  achieve transcendence in repose.
With no breeze to roust them,
  leaves on trees
  sleep without whispers,
  their twitch and flutter that of a dog's
  chasing bucks in a slumbrous hunt.
A spirit - a vision - a doe,
  cloaked in morning mist,
  steps slowly, nervously
  through dewy grass,
  like a virgin on her wedding night,

venturing farther than usual.
Thick with evening dreams
  I peer into morning's womb:
     generations teeming
     sleeping yet,
     as I must be
     nestled in this fog,
  the brink of life
  still hours away.

-*Heidi Juel*

Heidi Juel is a Professor of English at Austin Community College (Texas). She teaches Honors courses in Magical Realism, and Native North America. Writing is her passion, second only to inspiring students to value the power of words as an expression of self, and an outlet in times of need.

# A Letter From Israel

I miss you so much
My poet
I miss Oslo.
You come to visit me,
Like a platonic figure
Longing
For a woman who lost the
Catharsis
In a city with no drawing,
With a man stuck with a broken foot
Responding
To the celebration of the woman that I am
And the women here named the same
Perfume over ten years
While I named (at the same time)
The same pills.

This is my accompaniment
I can not beautify
My life
As you can't either.
So I'm eating you

A little too much – sometimes with
My ripeness.

With my clouded eyebrows
And a cigarette in
My mouth

You wear the Kippah that I bought you
With Norwegian letters
Spelling your name

There is no better tribute here
My love,
This is
Israel.

-*Tali Cohen Shabtai*

Tali Cohen Shabtai, is a poet she was born in Jerusalem, Israel Tali began writing poetry at young age of six, she was an excellent literature student. She began Publishing her impressions in the school's newspaper. She first published her poetry in a respectful literature magazine in Israel the "Moznayim" at age 15.

Tali is the author of three poetry books: "Purple diluted in a black's thick " bilingual 2007, "Protest" bilingual 2012, "Nine years away from you"2018, Two of her books are bilingual , and the third book "Nine years from you" is scheduled to be published in foreign edition abroad. Tali's poems express spiritual and physical exile. Cohen is studying her exile and freedom paradox, Her cosmopolitan vision is very obvious in her writing Cohen Shabtai lived years in Oslo Norway, the USA

# Ransom Note Typed on an Old Underwood with an "O" That Won't Strike

N  W LISTEN UP, D  L  RES!!!

BY N  W Y  U KN  W THAT Y  UR PRIZE
P    DLE IS MISSING.
WE G  T HER AND N    P WERS
 N EARTH CAN TAKE HER FR  M US.
S   D  N'T EXPECT T   SEE PENEL  PE AGAIN
IF Y  U PUT THE C  PS HUNTING F  R HER.
RIGHT N  W SHE'S IN AN   LD B  X
WITH A SQUEAK T  Y F  R C  MPANY
BUT SHE'LL BE G    D AS CAN BE
IF Y  U F  LL W   UR INSTRUCTI  NS T   THE LETTER.
Y  U WILL BE C  NTACTED AT   NE  'CL  CK T M RR W
WHERE T   DELIVER $10,000 IN   LD BILLS
F  R HER SAFE RETURN.
D  N'T BE STUPID AND MAKE THIS
PUBLIC   R I SWEAR WE WILL BE F  RCED
T  SH  T THE P   CH!
REMEMBER WE ARE PLENTY SMART GUYS!!!

Y  URS IN CHRIST,

AN  NYM  US

*-Terry Allen*

Terry Allen is an Emeritus Professor of Theatre Arts at the University of Wisconsin-Eau Claire, where he taught acting, directing and playwriting. He is the author of the chapbook Monsters in the Rain (Kelsay Books, 2019). His poems have appeared in many journals, including I-70 Review, Freshwater Poetry Journal, Chariton Review, Third Wednesday, Star 82 Review, Dime Show Review, Popshot Quarterly, Cloudbank, Into the Void and Main Street Rag.
My ripeness.

# You are the incense

breath elastic that swirls a vigil through my night
gathers my ashes to resurrect me with dawn
the sacrifice yet to stay dead, condemned to live
another day
climb mountain streets of anguish and laughter
untangle so many histories, so much like my own
with nails that would hold us to their sorrows
drown there without ever having tasted just a drop
of bliss
kind breezes blow away cardboard cross beams
released we sigh relieved, walk into what feels
like freedom, the kind we read in books, hear
from pulpits, pundits, political ego gods who promise
to take care of us if we vote for them who know what
to do because they wear rich, 4-button suits
bosses who promise raises then seem to forget but
not the myriad excuses they memorize from foxy-
locksy news, police more military than neighborly
magistrates who only know one word for the
little people, "guilty" but for the Lincoln chauffeured
a pass
little else from radio, tv, too many redacted teacher syllabi
words that wine and dine us, make us feel good
the words we memorized, got an "A" for, yet the price is
emptiness
that bitter stomach ache that leaves us restless

unsure, wanting someone to save us, a hero to make
everything better, when the better grows gaunt locked
in prisons of frozen hearts, so
the peeled orange has no fruit
we find nothing in our hands after all our obedience
we walk barking streets, cram into work spaces of
blistered dreams
stumble through weary darkness, try to smile, but
laughter has locked itself in the bathroom, a protest
against another calling day filled with shame, more
miserable from an unquenchable grief
that disturbing feel of dis-regard, failure, impotence
to change anything but one's underwear
awakened finally to realize a world wrapped up
in itself cannot see beyond, cannot feel beyond
its own greed for satisfaction, since one finally
recognizes in the face glaring back from the mirror
the awareness of being used, never loved only
taken advantage of, left to figure out what other
sandwich to make since the bologna is gone and
only peanut butter remains, someone else scooped out
the last remains of jelly from the welches' jar
the quiet culprit sits innocently quiet… watching cartoons
still, you are the incense, breath elastic that swirls
a vigil through the night, patient, since you can only
be a presence to massage consciousness for humane
action, the dissolution of fabricated differences that
splinter others from the care of what could be for all
resurrected into knowledge of the truth, so simple, yet

so difficult to melt the concrete enclaves created for
those only born to serve no matter what crayola shade
they show up as, no matter what societal space they
have been corralled into as if to watch an action
adventure movie, starring themselves as the ones who
fight and die so others can rock on their distant porches
laughing as they sip their bourbon, and the ones left
look up to them wishing they could be there with them
When their own lives sink into the grave they dug for themselves,
unaware they were born to be the sacrifice resurrected
by the dawn, unless they wake up feel the presence in their
bones, their flesh
their bodies that relate to all bodies, all flesh, all bones
since, the Presence loves them all, and loving will
wait till they are ready to die to the Lie and become Real

-*Jeff Cannon*



Jeff Cannon: author of Intimate Witness: The Carol Poems (2009), Eros Faces of Love and Finding the Father at Table (2010). I was an ever-present attendee (until recently due to health issues) at the "Dirty Gerund Poetry Show" at Ralph's Diner: my poetry home for 11years. Other publishing credits include Goose River Anthology (2009 & 2014) and Boundless (2014). Upcoming Another Year of Living Under the Dragon Stars and Heart Rants for Conscience Sake.

# My God

My God
Is that drop dead gorgeous kid
That you never noticed
In front of you
In the line
Outside the club
That the door guy
Lets in
Then
At the last minute
Turns to you and your friend
And says
"Oh, they're with me, too- no cover charge."

Then, once you're in
You never see again

-PW Covington


PW Covington writes in the beat tradition of the North American highway.
In 2019 his short fiction collection "North Beach and Other Stories" was named a LGBTQ Fiction Finalist by the International Book Awards. Covington lives in Albuquerque, NM. Follow him on Instagram @BeatPW.

# Seyewailo
# (Yaqui: Flower World)

*The Indians of the Isles (Choctaw Indians) wondered whether the newly arrived Spaniards were gods or men, while the whites wondered whether the indigenous peoples were human or animal. -- Pierre Clastres, Archeology of Violence*

*What we did in the 1960s and early 1970s was raise the consciousness of white America that this government has a responsibility to Indian people. That there are treaties; that textbooks in every school in America have a responsibility to tell the truth. An awareness reached across America that if Native American people had to resort to arms at Wounded Knee, there must really be something wrong. And Americans realized that native people are still here, that they have a moral standing, a legal standing. From that, our own people began to sense pride. -- Dennis Bank*

In the cold of February 27, 1973
The caravans of people rolled
Into symbolic Pine Ridge Reservation
Men, women, locals, urban Indians
And American Indian Movement members
Headed to hallowed ground
It was the site of the last massacre of the Indian Wars
Wounded Knee!

It was a full moon
Dark and scary

There was the sense
that a battle was forthcoming
Many of these young men
Had committed themselves to-to die.

I had children
I had to do whatever
It took
For them I could
Make a stand.

We were seen as
As a destructive agents
Cause we traveled
in the safety of caravans
With our Molotov Cocktails.

The obliteration of our culture
Our spiritual ways
Our entire way of being
Was on the verge of being
Stamped out.

If there was a smoke signal
It was that a band of Indians
Took on the government
It was in the spirit of our
Elders; Crazy Horse,
And ourselves.

On TV the narrator
Relegated us to a
Strange story from the wilderness
From that sacred place
Our ancestor went to pull
The new imaginary.

A group of Indians
Had overthrown the town
Of Wounded Knee in South Dakota.
And that we were in charge.

We were angry
Over the poverty of deprivation
From the loss of our land
Our language
From our inability
To continue to be Indians.

They wanted our bodies
But only in the image
Of the colonizer
Not our hair
Our braids
Our cradle boards

We had been deprived
Deprived in the enclosure

Of modernity
Of the enlighten
Master signifier
The empty signifier
Of a regime of signification
That wanted the land
The earth and its treasures
Wanted the Indian's body
Only as material substrate
To exploit in the demise
And disposition of the earth
And its richness.

In the suburbs of Los Angeles
I watched on TV
With my father
His brown Yaqui skin
His stoic sensibility
His love for my
Hybrid disposition.

I felt something
Burning in me
What it was
Made me angry
At the images on the screen.

I never forgot
That fire that lit in my blood

Why simple images
Of people like me
Would trigger something
So ancient in me.

I felt the wilderness
And the flowery world
Burst in me.
Where was this
Seyewailo, this flowery world.

In the suburbs of LA
It was nowhere
How did it manage to reignite?
Where was it hiding?

We had been shunned
Forced to disappear
To be never seen
No reminders of the past
Of the love of the "Surem"
and Yomumuli our mother.

I could not find the
Saila maso, our little brother deer
In the artificial facade of Los Angeles
The sea ania (a place of complete beauty and harmony)
Was leaking in
And I didn't know from where.

Was it buried in the
Interstitial spaces of my DNA
In a place some may call the wilderness
The wilderness of the surem
Of my ancestors
A place out of reach beyond the
Demagogic rules of the
Dominant signifier

As i went through school
That wilderness
That sea ania grew in me
I desired the justice
Yomumuli had
Wanted for our people
At Tosai Bwia"white earth"
Where she rumbled the tree
For the "Sure", our people.

That enchanted world, "yo ania"
That burst from within me
Has given me the gift
Of critical reasoning.

Those elders along the way
Have help me trace
The source of that rumbling
That has so disturbed our communities.

The Vine Deloria's
And so many communities
Have created the "sea ania"
That is my life of fighting for justice

I have loved the youth
In the same manner
That so many others
Had helped me along the way.

I have become the "yo ania",
That enchanted place
For the new generation.

The institutions that have
Leveraged my gifts
Have tried to moderate
That fire burning in my blood

There is no way
To quench that desire for the wilderness
For the enchanted places in my being
While saila maso
Leads my escape with his footprints
I follow the jus bellum

If there is to be justice
Then I am that Mulier.

In the manner that
The old ones have
Spread across the world
I have touched and fired
The inner "yo anias" and "sea anias"
Of those who have learned from me.

If the "Surem" are to spread
Across communities
It must be in the manner
Of recreating "the wilderness"
And the "enchanted places"
Of our ancestors.

The "yo anias" and "sea anias"
Cannot be repressed by
Any dominant regime of signification
Nor any imposed dominant signifiers
Especially those that hope to shatter
The magic of the people
And the community.

I am that sacredness
Both enchanted and sacred
That justice that refuses
To be silenced
That will forever continue
To rumble at the edges

Of any dominant
Fossilization...
I am that rumbling
That enchantment
That fire hidden
In the interstitial spaces
Of my ancestors DNA.

-*Tezozomoc*

Tezozomoc is a Los Angeles Chicano Poet and 2009 Oscar Nominated Activist and has been published by Floricanto Press, "Gashes!: Poems and Pain from the halls of injustice", a collection of poetry, ISBN-13: 978-1951088040, 9/2019. He has also been published in the following journals: The Oddball Magazine, 06/19/2019. Spitpoetzine, Volume 6, 6/15/2019. The Silver Stork, silverstorkmagazine.weebly.com/, 2018.

# Menstruation Hay(na)ku

When I bleed
I camouflage
tears

-*Eileen R. Tabios*

Eileen R. Tabios has released about 60 collections of poetry, fiction, essays, and experimental biographies from publishers in ten countries and cyberspace. Most recently, she released a short story collection, PAGPAG: The Dictator's Aftermath in the Diaspora and a poetry collection, The In(ter)vention of the Hay(-na)ku: Selected Tercets 1996-2019. The inventor of the hay(na)ku, a 21st century diasporic poetic form, she has seen her writing and editing works receive recognition through awards, grants and residencies. More information is available at http://eileenrtabios.com

# Shades of Meaning

    ghosts appear behind words
        sometimes atop them

    why should words
    overlap
    in meaning?

    isn't that
    inefficient
    for language
    as a tool?

    but if language
    is an art –
    and words
    a palette to
    choose from

    in the undertone
    and under
    tow, ghosts
    are hiding

    not for long

*-Jim LaVilla-Havelin*

Jim LaVilla-Havelin is the author of five books of poetry. WEST, poems of a place was published by Wings Press is 2017. LaVilla-Havelin is the San Antonio Coordinator for National Poetry Month, Poetry Editor for the San Antonio Express-News/Houston Chronicle, and the 2019 City of San Antonio Awardee of Distinction in the Arts for Literary Arts.

# We Could Not Know

No, we could not know.

Our tiny antennae reached out, trembling, hoping for a message,

clear advice on how to help. We were stunned

by the smallness of our worlds.

Here is the edge of your street,

three scrappy leaves. From which tree did they fall?

Here, the wrapper from someone else's gum.

I could pick up trash without seeing anyone.

No one would breathe on us

in the iron chair back of the house,

beside the bamboo. Machines to connect us

to the outside world. And now we would eat applesauce

from cups, bake a batch of biscuits, feel the quiet

settling down like a sheen of future disappearances

when no one will answer the number we call.

-*Naomi Shihab Nye*

Naomi Shihab Nye was born in St. Louis, Missouri. Her father was a Palestinian refugee and her mother an American of German and Swiss descent, and Nye spent her adolescence in both Jerusalem and San Antonio, Texas. She earned her BA from Trinity University in San Antonio. Nye is the recipient of numerous honors and awards for her work, including the Ivan Sandrof Award for Lifetime Achievement from the National Book Critics Circle, the Lavan Award, the Paterson Poetry Prize, the Carity Randall Prize, the Isabella Gardner Poetry Award, the Lee Bennett Hopkins Poetry award, the Robert Creeley Prize, and many Pushcart Prizes. She has received fellowships from the Lannan Foundation, the Guggenheim Foundation, and she was a Witter Bynner Fellow. From 2010 to 2015 she served as a Chancellor of the Academy of American Poets. In 2018 she was awarded the Lon Tinkle Award for Lifetime Achievement from the Texas Institute of Letters. Nye is the Poetry Foundation's Young People's Poet Laureate

# Como Hubiera

Como hubiera
querido quererte aún
mejor y entender que
la frontera reflejada en
tu quijada dura
en tu boca fuerte
a veces en la sonrisa
tan sincera como
la de tus padres
sí era traspasable

Como hubiera
querido decir que
el viaje sin remedio
lo hiciste por un amor
vivo, tangible y real
y no solo hecho de
las puras palabras

Como hubiera
querido hacerte
entender que mi
sangre tambien
vive en tu país
la fuente de mis
antepasados y

todos los sueños
como alas de
un papalotl de
papel china

Como hubiera
querido cruzar
la frontera final
a tu lado sin los
mismos miedos o
el eco sanguinario
de fantasmas viejas
clavadas en mis
venas desde antes
cuando aun existia
dentro del vientre
de mi madre y contra
cuales he luchado
desde hace siglos

Como hubiera
querido ser bueno
ante tus ojos de
obsidiano y tus
pasos hacia el
mentado norte

Como hubiera
querido salvar

tanto a nuestro
cariño como hubiera
querido cicatrizar
a tanta gente con
sed perdida en
el desierto por
nada y sin nada
más que heridas
de lo inalcanzable

Como hubiera
querido tratar de
volar por el espacio
teleportarme a ti
y al pasado con
brazos cargados
de agua y pan para
aquellas esperanzas
y un beso profundo
plantado en tu frente

Como hubiera
querido despedirme
sin la desolación o
el diluvio de lágrimas
saladas sobre nuestros
recuerdos ya convertidos
en torres inmóviles

Como hubiera
querido borrar esas
leyes racistas y
xenofóbicas para
no impedir tu
camino por las
piedras minerales

Como hubiera
querido sentir el
viento de tus mil
caricias otra vez
Como hubiera
querido borrar
mi propia torpeza
y hacerte creer
que sobre todo
y para siempre
eres mi otro yo
in lak'ech

*-Abel Salas*

Based in Los Angeles, journalist and poet Abel Salas has written for The Austin Chronicle, Los Angeles Times Magazine, Los Angeles Magazine, LA Weekly and the New York Times, among others. His poems have appeared in Zyzzyva, Beltway Quarterly, Cutthroat: A Journal of the Arts, Cipactli and Huizache, Americas Review as well as the anthologies Poetry of Resistance: Voices for Social Change (University of Arizona Press, 2016) and The Coiled Serpent: Poets Arising From the Cultural Quakes and Shifts of Los Angeles (Tia Chucha Press, 2016). Internationally, his poems have appeared in the anthology Huellas a Través del Tiempo (Ajalpan, Pueblam SIPEA, 2014) and in the regional edition of Mexico's second largest national daily La Jornada (Zacatecas, Zacatecas) He is the editor and publisher of Brooklyn & Boyle, a community, arts and cultural monthly and was a co-founder of Corazón del Pueblo, a grass-roots arts, education and political action center in Boyle Heights.

# REMEMBERING MOTHER

Left arm
Left eye
Is throbbing

Remembering mother
Who whispers in the air
Beware

The water in the arum leaves
Would slip suddenly
Where do I find again

A wind is turning stronger
The arum leaf is shaking hard
Seeing it
The upset sea
Is having tide and ebb

The sea cannot flow by
Like the river
It is heaving up and down
Staying rooted to the spot.

-Guna Moran
*Translated from Assamese - Bibekananda Choudhury*

Guna Moran is an emerging Assamese poet and critic. His poems have been published in various international magazines, journals and anthologies.

# Way too Soon

The ceasing of breath
did not announce
(but I saw it cast its shadow on you
just a day before)
the lines that spiked, now lie flat
it all was silent now
no beeps or warning tones
to awaken those beside you.
Half-dead, half-alive.

I had stood
gazing at what had become
of the simple desires
that had shone in your eyes
not many needs
but morsels of time
we failed to spend.
Now hungry.

Those eyes never quite opened
for weeks you struggling lay
braving and fighting
torn between worlds
the gods of death
and those of us that lived.
You stirred not.

I know you are gone
but it is just a spell
next door somewhere you drift
in a world just like this one
or perhaps happier.
I hope.

The emptiness and shadows
gnaw slowly at the clock
the minute lingers for us
like a dew-drop waiting to fall
the days remain hollow
without your child-like curiosity.
And tantrums.
It will never be the same
you took the anchor away
we talk though and it rips me
when Daddy calls me by your name
though the curtains have fallen
we live to tell the tale.
Unforgotten.

© *Sandhya Suri*

About this piece –
I lost my mother to a fatal road accident. She was on the ventilator for 17 days before she succumbed to her severe injuries. I met her alive last the day before when I had one to visit her at the hospital. I was nursing my daughter who was also in the same accident and was bedridden with three pelvic fractures. This was written a day or so after she passed. This is my tribute to her.

Sandhya Suri is an Indian Navy Veteran who is now a Change Enabler and professional speaker. Her first co-authored political fiction will be out in June. She is an established poet and is now working on her second book which is about her life's experiential journey. Her belief system is a blend of ikigai, kintsugi and meraki. She currently lives in Delhi, India.

# Iluminado
*For my son Hawk Galván*

Your light
has not gone out
We are more
illuminated
by you than ever
You are a starburst
a galaxy of brilliance
covering us
with knowing
We mourn
your physical body
your voice
your infectious laughter
your sly and sure smile
That huge embrace
that comforted us
with all the wisdom
You are
We remember
We look out
over the bay you loved
Behind us
a stand of evergreen
trees nestled between
those that sleep
over winter

You are there
new in your Spirit form
perched at the highest point
For all to see
To reassure us
you've not gone
we just have
to remember
you are magic
Son

purest
soul. I ever
knew. You. Always. Happy.
From your mother's belly. Smiling.
Loving.

-Odilia Galván Rodríguez


Odilia Galván Rodríguez poet, writer, editor, publisher, and activist, is the author of six volumes of poetry. Her latest book, from FlowerSong Books is The Color of Light ~ Poems to the Mexica and Orisha Energies. She is also co-editor, along with the late Francisco X. Alarcón, of the award-winning anthology Poetry of Resistance: Voices for Social Justice, The University of Arizona Press. She has worked as the editor for several magazines, most recently at Tricontinental Magazine in Havana, Cuba and Cloud Women's Quarterly Journal online.

# Son

purest
soul. I ever
knew. You. Always. Happy.
From your mother's belly. Smiling.
Loving.

-*Odilia Galván Rodríguez*

Odilia Galván Rodríguez poet, writer, editor, publisher, and activist, is the author of six volumes of poetry. Her latest book, from FlowerSong Books is The Color of Light ~ Poems to the Mexica and Orisha Energies. She is also co-editor, along with the late Francisco X. Alarcón, of the award-winning anthology Poetry of Resistance: Voices for Social Justice, The University of Arizona Press. She has worked as the editor for several magazines, most recently at Tricontinental Magazine in Havana, Cuba and Cloud Women's Quarterly Journal online.

# Pam

So brave of you friend
With what you said
The journey closing
The end is ahead

What strength you have
Battling through the fight
Increasingly tough days
Pondering if another, each night

While the journey done well
It was your strength to share
In the end I admire
Appreciating friends' prayers

Without using the words
I heard your goodbye
Gratitude, hopefulness
You exemplify

This is my prayer
As you transition above
Your mind at peace
Heart full of love

-Doug Croft

Doug Croft journals poetry and essays. His work has previously appeared in several anthologies and poetry magazines. He has also written five sketches which have been performed in various settings.

# The Elevator at a Hispanic Serving University

My profé from Califas said it was the graffiti that convinced her she would be at home on this campus. She said it was during her interview when she realized she wanted this South Texas job–

when she noticed that someone (most likely a bored student alone

on their ride) had removed the third letter "E" and final letter "R" with a marker permanently leaving "EL VATO " behind– to welcome each bilingual passenger on their way to and from class.

-Amalia Ortiz




Amalia Ortiz appeared on three seasons of Def Poetry on HBO. NBC Latino named her first book of poetry, Rant. Chant. Chisme., one of "10 Great Latino Books of 2015." She is a CantoMundo Fellow and received an MFA in Creative Writing from UTRGV. In 2019, she was awarded a NALAC Grant to film music videos for her latest book The Cancion Cannibal Cabaret - a post-apocalyptic punk rock musical- published by Aztlan Libre Press.

# Herencias Herreranáuticas

y si maestro… I am running hard into the stoic winds of a time before, before the quasar manifesto in a mission split-posterized memory like the fire, which bled from a thousand veins strewn across the remnants of a tomorrow dawn dream. i want to sing and cry or laugh and die until the whispering stones awaken. si, maestro… years ago cuando te conocí y empezaba a leer (francisco me había dado una copia de sudor de pueblos). i was born beyond the event horizon and at ten was marching alongside my siblings. simultáneamente escuchaba ya a las lecturas de black elk. mine was a midwife generation that attended the birth of cyberpunk, and smiled knowingly. marvel comics & the x-men. luego los hermanos hernández y sus love and rockets. my wayward spiral climb on fictitious concrete spires. tus poemas me alibibabiaban (alivianaban) y después llegué a ver y conocer a los demás, algunos de tus contemporáneos; lorna dee-francisco-juanalicia-rodrigo. you were wearing camouflage. i'm was on the bildungsroman ride to individuality sedición/seducción por y con la querida poesía. starstruck by a wandering fever using scholarship funds surreptitiously. feeling alive and alien, old before I was young, tasting implausibility with a spoon I pilfered during the denouement of deconstructionism.

so I buried myself once more in the barrio where I learned de colores, bridging an ancient chasm beneath the fervent visions arching into the hyperbolic moment where the consensual hallucinations begin like the germination of another dialectic where polar ends reverse themselves unexpectedly at irregular bursts like beacons on a haywire trip through shellfish netting and sentient kelp.

aquí en el barrio... el eastside where a few berets still imagine an aztlan liberated (with the help of unnamed accomplices). aquí donde nacieron ciegos cinco gatitos. i slept with the cinnamon reek of feline wisdom behind those tiny, clouded eyes. i stumble on the accordion keys and still read los cuentos policiacos... in between territorios y el otro... la vuelta al día en ochenta mundos. my sanity caught in mid-swallow. i sit and stare as the hormigas diligently erect yet another painting; there are three lovely masterpieces already completed, lucid caverns unfolding as cuaduro's assassinator pincelazos dance wickedly around my living room couch. can I be accused of hermeticism? can I say nirvana and body count define my cultural paradigm? ¿gritaré que botellita de jerez, caifanes y el tri de la onda music in the lap of disenfranchised urban urchindom? ¿podría pronunciar cuerodeltamborhuehuetl o quizas teatro de crueldad?

puede ser que si. y todo se debe a esta liberación encontrada entre páginas herreranáuticas. because of you, i eat rich writers for lunch and carry the banner of sandinismo in every follicle y si, maestro, espero que un día tomaremos un café en el este de los ángeles. lloraré con alegría y la tristeza del hijo perdido, bereft of so many mothers and fathers and brothers and sisters who graced the canvas of my life with such voluminous beauty before joining each other in mictlan or moving so far away.

día de las madres. Austin, 1992

-*Abel Salas*

Based in Los Angeles, journalist and poet Abel Salas has written for The Austin Chronicle, Los Angeles Times Magazine, Los Angeles Magazine, LA Weekly and the New York Times, among others. His poems have appeared in Zyzzyva, Beltway Quarterly, Cutthroat: A Journal of the Arts, Cipactli and Huizache, Americas Review as well as the anthologies Poetry of Resistance: Voices for Social Change (University of Arizona Press, 2016) and The Coiled Serpent: Poets Arising From the Cultural Quakes and Shifts of Los Angeles (Tia Chucha Press, 2016). Internationally, his poems have appeared in the anthology Huellas a Través del Tiempo (Ajalpan, Pueblam SIPEA, 2014) and in the regional edition of Mexico's second largest national daily La Jornada (Zacatecas, Zacatecas) He is the editor and publisher of Brooklyn & Boyle, a community, arts and cultural monthly and was a co-founder of Corazón del Pueblo, a grass-roots arts, education and political action center in Boyle Heights.

# Weightless

I've lost 11 pounds since you left.
I wasn't even trying. I just did.
I forgot to cook an entire breakfast
of bacon and sausage and 2 fried eggs
with fresh-grated hash browns and
a slice of butter-laden toast or
a biscuit smothered in gravy
served every single morning.

I've lost 27 pounds since you left.
Somehow I forgot to make a lunch
of a red meat, a starch, the starchiest
starch I could find, a veggie or
two cooked in lard, and maybe a
fruit covered in sugar and stuffed
inside a crust with butter and eggs.
Followed by a complete supper of
the same, yet different, configuration.

I've lost 42 pounds since you left.
Suddenly I wasn't tied to the stove
and the sink hand washing dishes
six times a day between meals which
better not include fish or chicken
or a nice salad as a side. When I
stepped out of the kitchen and

away from your expectations,
your demands, I walked into my own life.

I've lost 205 pounds since you left.
And I don't even miss you.
Not one little bit.

-*Karen Tardiff*

Karen has been writing since she could hold a pen. Her works can be seen in print and online, including Nowhere Poetry & Flash Fiction, Tuck Magazine, Ampersand Literary, Pif Magazine, Unlikely Stories, and The Dead Mule. She founded the Aransas County Poetry Society. Her e-book is Stumbling to Breathe.

# Juan Romero and the Dead Kennedy

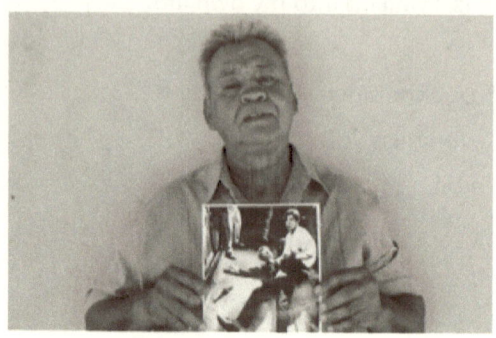

My name is Juan Romero
And I have this terrible secret
That i have had to live with
For the last 50 years.

Some would say
That I killed the last
Kennedy boy.
The smart kennedy boy

Not the Teddy
Nor the Johnny
But the Bobby

For many years
I could not look
At the pictures taken
By LA Times photographer Boris Yaro

It was too traumatic
Too much guilt
To be the Mexican
That killed Bobby.

The letters
Sent to the Ambassador Hotel
Addressed to the "bus boy"
They use to tell me
If you had not shaken
His hand he would
Still be alive
His blue eyes
Would still shine
And that perfect white
Smile would grace us.

But I had to stick
My hand it front of him
And shake it
Someone I admired
Someone who fought
For justice
For the poor
And downtrodden

I have been accused
Of being selfish
Why couldn't I had

Been a good mexican
And kept my head down
And sight away?

In 2010
I bought a suit
I had never owned
A suit before
It felt tight
Scratchy
But when I stood
In front of Bobby's gravestone
I felt tall
His values made me feel tall

And I had gone there
To ask his forgiveness
To be forgiven
For being the cause of his death

I felt like
He was proud of me
Cause i had lived
According to his values
I had been a good family man
A good father
A good husband
And I wanted his atonement.

As I shook his hand
I remember the
Weight of his body
Fall on the concrete floor
Of the hotel kitchen

I cupped my hand
Behind his head
Felt the warm blood
Trickle through
My fingers.

He was still
Murmuring
And I lowered my head
And he whispered,
"Is everyone okay?",
I stuttered a heavy, "Yes"

I had a Rosary
In my pocket
And pulled it out
And wrapped it around
His right hand
I thought he would
Need it more than I.
Quickly, they whisked
Him away.

He was gone
But my guilt
Persisted for over 50 years

*-Tezozomoc*

Tezozomoc is a Los Angeles Chicano Poet and 2009 Oscar Nominated Activist and has been published by Floricanto Press, "Gashes!: Poems and Pain from the halls of injustice", a collection of poetry, ISBN-13: 978-1951088040, 9/2019. He has also been published in the following journals: The Oddball Magazine, 06/19/2019. Spitpoetzine, Volume 6, 6/15/2019. The Silver Stork, silverstorkmagazine.weebly.com/, 2018.

# At the Fine Arts Gallery

Femur, mandible. Pelvic bone. Vertebrae: deer cemetery.
Rusted color-gone Chevy. Sepia ghosts carry on.
A rat snake, long, chin raised, its den nearby.
Water from a rock face, framed by ferns.
Blackfoot daisies. Winecups.
Cottonwoods in wind-animated dialog.
A private plane, intrusive drone.
Shotgun shells, scattered. Red.
Black vulture, downed, carrion for kin.
Silent scene of beaver work.
Rodent skull, hip high on a juniper tree.
White vertebra grins from a rear view mirror.
Stark landscape. A pickup truck, the vanishing point.

-*Heidi Juel*

Heidi Juel is a Professor of English at Austin Community College (Texas). She teaches Honors courses in Magical Realism, and Native North America. Writing is her passion, second only to inspiring students to value the power of words as an expression of self, and an outlet in times of need.

# Winter Road

Across from the moon-streaked
fields I took the winter road,
a joyous fountain near the entrance
even at this time of year, lampposts
lit up in the night in front of every
home, a lasting memory for me
ever since I moved here. No icy
wind, only a peaceful stillness,
and I listened to the silence, before
me the earth's white edge of sleep,
the heart of November, and I imagine
a carnation birthed in the lustrous
snow – blooming, every white petal
delicately unfolding.

-Bobbi Sinha-Morey

Bobbi Sinha-Morey lives a peaceful life at home, exploring the life around her to draw from, and being inspired by people she comes to know. She loves focusing on human nature and the experiences she's had, be they good or bad.

# Ausencia
*Para chubis*

Quisiera olvidar el olor de tu cuello.
El sonido de tu risa,
ruidoso como los mariachis que tocan en la plaza,
contagioso como los aplausos después.
Quisiera olvidar tus dedos elegantes que pueden tocar la guitarra
y yo
con sencillez.
Quisiera olvidar esa vez que bailamos en el metro,
delante del viejo ciego, el joven vendiendo rosas,
la niña sonriendo.
Quisiera olvidar tus abrazos,
fuertes y largas que duraban por la eternidad,
pero la eternidad entre tus brazos era muy corta.
Quisiera olvidar tu voz,
tu acento distincto,
el timbre que caliente mi sangre.
Mi corazón.
Quisiera olvidar tus ojos,
un dulce café,
tierna como la lluvia
que moja la tierra después de un dia caloroso.
Quisiera olvidar tantas cosas.
Quisiera olvidar nuestras conversaciones.
Miradas que dijo nada pero todo.
Promesas. Mares. Penguinos. Sonrisas. La luna. Verde.

Finlandia. San Blas. Ninjas. Limones. Cellos. Lagrimas.
Tu.
Quisiera olvidar...
pero necesito recordar.

*-Lea Colchado*

Lea Christine Colchado is a lover of words and stories, especially from Chicanas. She currently is a Rhetoric and Composition graduate student at Texas State University where she explores and plays with the power of words, language, and identity.

# Aberrant Thought While in a Check-out Line

It's okay to cry or smile in private,
but if among others, even strangers,
displaying our mood is at best
bad manners, and at worst
demented behavior to be evaded.

But would it not be simpler to cope
if we blatantly screamed or sulked
or laughed out loud for no apparent cause?
For we could sense the frames of mind
of all those nearest to us,
and hug or hide.

-Edward Ahern

Ed Ahern resumed writing after forty odd years in foreign intelligence and international sales. He's had over two hundred fifty stories and poems published so far, and five books. Ed works the other side of writing at Bewildering Stories, where he sits on the review board and manages a posse of six review editors.
https://twitter.com/bottomstripper
https://www.facebook.com/EdAhern73/?ref=bookmarks
https://www.instagram.com/edwardahern1860/

# LONG EL PASO AFTERMATH

She kisses stillness—open-eyed, awake—
a soft lash brushes her always damp cheek
and teases life to open lips. Each day
begins like this before a working week
unfolds, long, before her. It's hard to make
breakfast—alone—again—lost in vast time,
deserted, with ruined pictures—face down—
on dark tables. Names slip away like lines
on her made up face. She still wants to miss
everyone—everything—but alarms sound
to shatter stillness in her sheets and this
sorrow's all she has, draped across her floor.
She knows it will stay until she begins to miss
grief. Knowing they're gone. Knowing nothing more.

-Mark Mitchell

Mark J. Mitchell was born in Chicago and grew up in southern California. His latest poetry collection, Starting from Tu Fu was just published by Encircle Publications.
He is very fond of baseball, Louis Aragon, Miles Davis, Kafka and Dante. He lives in San Francisco with his wife, the activist and documentarian, Joan Juster where he makes his meager living pointing out pretty things. He has published 2 novels and three chapbooks and two full length collections so far. Titles on request. A meager online presence can be found at https://www.facebook.com/MarkJMitchellwriter/

# I Remember the Alamo (Differently)

Do you remember the Alamo
Cause I remember
Learning about the Alamo
Like I remember being a little kid
And being told go back to Mexico
Do you remember the Alamo
Cause I remember
Learning about the Alamo
Like I remember being a little kid
And being told
Go back to Mexico and eat your tacos
Like I remember
Learning about the Alamo

You hear it all the time
I am not a racist
I just believe in the rule of law
What part about illegal don't you get
What I don't get
Is how the same people
Who backed the Iraqi invasion
Now want to complain
About something called
Illegal immigration
You know folks being in places
They don't belong

These people want to talk
About the illegality of immigrants
The criminality of workers
Well I have a list of criminals
I feel never should have left home
Their names were Jefferson, Madison, Monroe
Monroe where are your documents
You hear it all the time
If they were real men
They would stay in their own country and fix it
Yet
When the Mexican presidential election
Was stolen in two thousand six
The people shut down the capital for five months
Bush stole not one but two elections
And we didn't do shit
Don't tell me Mexicans don't know how to fight
That same year
Hundreds of thousands if not millions
Of Mexicans poured into American streets
In protests organized in less than two weeks
Don't tell me Mexicans don't know how to organize
And don't tell me all this talk is divisive
Because unless you're a racist
My pride is not divisive
Unless you are a racist
My dignity is not divisive
Because otherwise
You're actually arguing

I should be without it
And another thing
My family, my community
We are not an ethnic study
We are a course in human history
Because we are as real
And as valid
And as universal
As anybody
So for anyone who would say to me
That it is divisive
Or worse yet racist
When I say I am proud to be Latino
Well get ready motherfucker
Because I say this
From Caracas
To the Pampas
To the Chiapas
To East Los Angeles
From the lowliest paid dishwasher
In the loneliest café
In the northernmost tip of Maine
All the way down south
To the southernmost cone of Argentina
Wherever there are so many as one of us
I say viva viva viva America Latina
Now there are some
Who would tell you
That this is hate speech

Nonsense
I love everybody
So long as they remain lovely
But wait a minute man
The minute you start breaking
Up families
Or calling our children anchor babies
Then yeah
We got some problems
Because I hate racism
And I hate economic imperialism
And I hate transnational capitalism
Because I am a communist
Soy un comunista
And I make no more apologies for that
Than I do for being Mexican
But yeah these people aren't racist
They just believe in the rule of law
What part of illegal don't you get
Yet
Go to any one of their rallies
And you will hear things like
Go back to Mexico
Do your drugs
Eat your tacos
Or some really off the wall shit like
Remember the Alamo
Well I do remember the Alamo
Like I remember the Dien Bien Phu

Like I remember the Tet Offensive
Like I remember the battle of little BigHorn
And the wars of Pontiac
Like I remember Nat Turner's midnight ride
Like I remember when Cubans and Angolans
Shot the forces of Apartheid from African skies
At the battle of Cuito Cuanavale
Like I remember the Alamo
Like I remember Magellan's watery grave
Off the island of Mactan
When people not yet known as Filipinos
With no more than bamboo spears and bolos
Confronted Spanish conquistadors in steel plated armor
And drowned their asses in less than three feet of water
Like I remember the Alamo
Like I remember the Mexican Revolution
Like I remember the Haitian Revolution
Like I remember the Irish Revolution
Like I remember the Iranian Revolution
Like I remember the Algerian Revolution
Rocking the Casbah
Like I remember the Alamo
Like I remember the Cuban Revolution
Like I remember the Nicaraguan Revolution
Like I remember the Vietnamese Revolution
Like I remember the Chinese Revolution
Like I remember the Russian Revolution
Like I remember every piece of people's or anti colonial history
So yeah you racist sack of shit

I do remember the Alamo
I just remember it a little differently

-*Matt Sedillo*

Matt Sedillo is a Chicano poet, writer, creative director, and public intellectual called "the poet laureate of the struggle" by Dr. Paul Ortiz and "the best political poet in America" by investigative journalist Greg Palast. He has been featured in over 80 colleges and universities and various media outlets including All Def Digital, Los Angeles Times, and C-SPAN. His collection "Mowing Leaves of Grass" (FlowerSong Press) was published in 2019.

# Claudia Patricia Gomez Gonzalez Is Returned To Mother Earth

At the border children cry in cages.

I wake drenched in dark dreams.

My mother reaches from the grave. Nails catch the hem of my dress.
I fall on granite. Red streaks my shins.

Wrapped in a gray Mayan shawl, her mother is silent.

My father sits sobbing. Dust spots his black suit. Dried red roses lay across his legs. Thorns pierce the wool.

Her father weeps.

#Claudia Patricia Gomez Gonzalez. #Say her name.

Just turned twenty. Taking flight from violence in Guatemala. Shot

in the head by a Texas border agent. May 23, 2018.
Mother and father receive the white coffin carrying their daughter.

Its cover lifted partway.

*-chella courington*

Chella Courington is a writer and teacher whose poems and stories appear in numerous anthologies and journals including Spillway, The Collagist, and The Los Angeles Review. Her novella, Adele and Tom: The Portrait of a Marriage, is forthcoming from Breaking Rules Publishing. Originally from the Appalachian South, Courington lives in California with another writer.

# Issues of:

Because it is an issue of labor
in maquiladoras
in China
in fast food kitchens
in Kentucky coal mines
in sweatshops
in outsourced "American" factories

Because it is an issue of class
for the 99%
for old money and new
for those famous for being famous
for the working poor
for nacos and fresas
for mirreyes and inmigrantes
for those on this and that side of a wall
for those stuck in the school to prison pipeline

Because it is an issue of human rights
for slain activists
for the silenced
for the tortured
for the unjustly imprisoned
for the slaughtered tribes
over stolen lands and resources

Because it is an environmental issue
in the Rio Grande
in Fukushima
in the overfished oceans
along the Gulf coast
beneath the fracked earth
for the lush golf courses
in the midst of drought

Because it is an issue of gender
at Hobby Lobby
reflected
in the sexualization of women
in pay inequality
in the glass ceiling
in reproduction control
in the enslavement of female bodies
and femicide

Because it is an issue of race
in Ferguson
at the border checkpoint
for those stopped and frisked
reflected
in pay inequality
in the glass ceiling
in reproduction control
in the enslavement of brown bodies
and genocide

Because it is an issue of corporate greed
Because it is an issue of exploitation
Because it is an issue of corruption

Because it is a global issue—
the commodification and
control of the planet—

it is the fight of our lives

-Amalia Ortiz

Amalia Ortiz appeared on three seasons of Def Poetry on HBO. NBC Latino named her first book of poetry, Rant. Chant. Chisme., one of "10 Great Latino Books of 2015." She is a CantoMundo Fellow and received an MFA in Creative Writing from UTRGV. In 2019, she was awarded a NALAC Grant to film music videos for her latest book The Cancion Cannibal Cabaret - a post-apocalyptic punk rock musical- published by Aztlan Libre Press.

# América para los americanos: Central America, 2016

They say we come back
como los mexicanos.
Acabados, sinvergüenzas,
sin chambas, sin muelas
Maje. That when the migra
dumps us back in Tegus
San Pedro, Huehue, Guate,
La Chureca, the campo o
dondequiera we can't stop
saying pinche, no mames
y vete a la chingada. They say

we dress too flashy. Chains,
boots and tatuajes. Gold
teeth and belt buckles. Como
cholos. Narcos. Asesinos.
They act like they don't
know that in México no
somos cheros. That they call
you cerote, while they kick
the shit out of you because
they know you are
centroamericano before

you can say paráte vos.
Like they don't know that

when you get to the U.S.
they don't call you Chapín
Catracho, Guanaco o Nica.
They call you wetback,
alien, bad hombre, illegal.
They kick the shit out of you
and say, "Don't speak
Mexican! Go home!
Make America Great Again!"

*-Abigail Carl-Klassen*

Abigail Carl-Klassen is a poet, writer, educator, translator, and activist on the U.S.-Mexico border. She earned her MFA from the University of Texas at El Paso's Bilingual Creative Writing Program. Her book, A'int Country Like You, is available from Digging Press.

# Perilous Borders

To search for freedom
And safety
Is a right as human beings
We all share.

I come from afar escaping
      Violence, corruption and poverty
Survival is my basic instinct
Buried deep within my soul.
I have left it all behind
      My country, home and loved ones.
I kissed my mother's cool forehead
That dismal morning in January
Bidding farewell to my greatest love
Gently touching her soft gray hair
I now remember with great nostalgia
Such immense somberness in her eyes
Which exuded the great uncertainty she felt
      Deep within her
Knowing she may never see me again.

I look at her photo that accompanies me
And feel her beloved presence
Which sustains me through this turmoil
I look ahead at the obscure border
      Not too far away

Not knowing what awaits me on the other side.

I look down
And kiss my mother's image
Wiping my heartfelt tears
And rising up to continue
Maintaining hope inside my heart
        This peril will all be worth it.

-*Vanessa Caraveo*

Vanessa Caraveo is an award-winning author and published poet who has been avidly involved in writing throughout the years. Her poetry has been published in various anthologies and organizations and she hopes to uplift the lives of others through her literary work through this noble craft.

# When I Wear Bob Kaufman's Eyes

pillows become marbleized pillars
    of tiger's teeth.

When I wear Bob Kaufman's eyes
polar bears drown in tar, singing
raga dirges until noxious fumes
stream green from their pointy ears.

When I wear Bob Kaufman's eyes
homeless shelter bunks swallow lonely
children, by morning only their skeletons
are left chattering.

When I wear Bob Kaufman's eyes
Hiroshima light bulbs pop around the
globe in cut time to signal SOS.

-Tom Murphy


Tom Murphy's books are: Pearl (Flower Song Press 2020), American History (Slough Press, 2017), co-edited Stone Renga (Tail Feather, 2017), chapbook, Horizon to Horizon (Strike Syndicate, 2015). Murphy is Langdon Review's 2020 Writer-In-Residence. Murphy is a committee member of the People's Poetry Festival of Corpus Christi.

# Brother Shaman

He started cutting the hair
around his ears and letting
a mohawk grow
until he could tie up
the thick, dark hair off his neck

He had been a revered teacher
long before
he asked me to set my intentions
for the new moon ceremony
or showed me how to light
sage bundles and palo santo sticks
to bless the sacred space, the self
before bouts of despondency had time to settle
we stomped demons on the ground, dancing
until the sun came up
over Makati, and then San Antonio

He gave me an amethyst stone
before I started a crystal collection
to help me land gently in new places, in my travels
he gathered feathers, leaves, and hike talks
then gifted them, sealed with love
he was my healer before he needed a title
he could dance, nightlong around the fire
stomping away past tormentors

in a healing dance

*-Sarah Joy Thompson*

Sarah Joy Thompson is a Filipina-American author, who spent her childhood and teenage years in the Philippines doing humanitarian projects and missionary work with her family. Thompson's poetry invites readers to reflect on love of family, the thrill of discovering oneself, and the circle of life – namely our connection to nature and its remote landscapes. Her poems have appeared or are forthcoming in Sagebrush Review, 100 Thousand Poets for Change San Antonio: Women SPEAK, Through Layered Limestone: a Texas Hill Country anthology of place, Voices de la Luna, Visions International, For Women Who Roar, Houston Chronicle, and the San Antonio Express-News. Thompson is the author of two poetry collections "The Everyday, the Mundane, and the Brave" (Finishing Line Press, 2019) and "Driving into Black Mountains" (FlowerSong Press, 2020).

# ALONE TOGETHER

1.

'I don't have time for this' I say
Nobody has the time
'I don't have time for this either', you say
Here we stand - both not having time for this
We don't want the drama
But the drama is here all the same
So, we will stay together both not having time for this
But having time to not have time for this
Take your corner and I will take mine
I stand alone, no I want to be alone
You want to be alone too
We both stand alone together

2.

Let's be alone together.
You are one and I am one
But we stopped being separate a long time ago
We are 'we'
So, it's okay if you don't have time for this
It's okay if you want to be alone
As long as we are alone together
We stay Alone. We. Together

*-Debra Ayis*

Debra Ayis has been published in over 100 anthologies and has been awarded for her work. She was most recently published in "Life at a Crossroads", the CUNY Killens Review of Arts & Letters - Fall/Winter 2019; and Heart of Flesh Literary Journal - Winter 2019. Her website is www.valiantscribe.com

# URETHRAL ROCKET

There are 43,845 reasons you should not eat
the shell of the lobster, the canned beans, snails
fresh from the dungheap but no matter how
many doomsday scenarios the advertisers,
the insurance companies, the Association
for Concerned Walruses put into your head,
you still like your meat raw in the center. Yes,
even the centipede sashimi, fire on the tongue
and visions of the hive mind in your dreams.

The command line sits in front of you, blinks.
You know it doesn't judge and yet somehow it
still feels personal, like the kind of denial one
can only suffer on a third Thursday when the moon
is obscuring Orion's beer gut and the manscapers
have walked off the job until they receive hazard
pay. You just stare daggers back, whistle "Wee
Willie Winkie" in the saddest of all keys.

-*Robert Beveridge*

Robert Beveridge (he/him) makes noise (xterminal.bandcamp.com) and writes poetry in Akron, OH. Recent/upcoming appearances in Collective Unrest, Cough Syrup, and Blood & Bourbon, among others.

# Despair

Blurred Views
Beyond a quarter mile
Depression worsens in the
Leaf litters of Fall
On the slope of a hill
An imprisoned rainbow

A miserably failed man
Walks down the street
With a shadow of epics

In the way out
A music rises
With weeping tune of
One who lost the country

In the void,
Silence uproots
A thunder,
Seizing the voice
A while,
Before the rain
A heart burns

Back then, walking alone
The pain spreads

Like a frightened snake.

-*Priya Unnikrishnan*

Priya Unnikrishnan, a writer from Kerala, India now resides in Texas,USA. Published two poetry books and a book of stories and contributed works to different publisher's collections, Newspapers and Magazines. Writes both in Malayalam (language of Kerala, India) and English. Poem published in International Magazine Culturecult.

# Homeless Man

Have you ever spoken to a homeless man filled with rancor?
Maybe, but probably not
Who wants to taunt the gods of cancer?
Like a gut shot
It takes a long time to fully bleed out
It might get on you like a bloody spout
Dare we misplace our limited empathy?
Dare we waste our exhausted sympathy?
What about cause and effect?
Are you so sure you got it in the right order?
Why look at such distaste in the face?
I'm not Jesus I'm not Gandhi I'm not mother Theresa
Oh, look, he's falling
He probably does drugs
It's appalling but what a pity
That his life is so shitty
Who said he deserves to make his choices?
What voices are these? Oh, please.
He may look feral and even wild
You know, he once was just a baby, a child

-Elliott Stegall

Elliott Stegall is a professor of the Humanities and English. He is the author of the screenplay "Hell Hath No Fury" and numerous scholarly essays on cinema, gender, and war. He has acted in the short films Fall of a Saga (2003), Sins of the Mother (2006), and Stranger Things (2008).

# Homelessness

*--In memory of Homero Gomez Gonzalez and Raul Hernandez Romero, protectors of El Rosario Monarch Butterfly Preserve*

I never knew that being homeless
could dry my mouth, my eyes,
my tongue, my heart. Everything
feels parched and petrified. I am a walking
drought. I breathe out dust. I scorch.
There is lead in my soles and my soul.
My wings have turned to stone.

Homero and Raul told the narcos
that there was no room for them
in El Rosario—this was the Monarchs'
homeland. There was only room for wings
of gold, clouds of milkweed. The drug lords
said the butterflies would only survive on a wing
and a prayer. Homero went missing first.
After his body was found at the bottom
of a well, Raul was found beaten to death.

Who will step up to cocoon what remains
of the Monarchs' Michoacan? Who will defend
the defenders, the defenseless? Who will defend flight
in these leaden days, in these days heavy as a coffin?
When our Environmental Defenders have become
as Endangered as the species they protect.

*-Lucinda Zamora-Wiley*

Lucinda is originally from San Antonio, Texas, but she is an RGV transplant of over twenty years now. She is a high school English teacher at The Science Academy of South Texas, and she is enjoying her twentieth year of teaching. Related to Elena Zamora O'Shea, author of El Mesquite, reading, writing, and teaching are in Lucinda's blood. A former student of Billy Collins and Sharon Olds, Lucinda's greatest honor and privilege is being the mother of revolutionary poet, Ava Sofia Zamora-Wiley.

# MY BODY AS A BACKPACK FOR LOVED ONES & THINGS THAT SIT ON A WHEELCHAIR

Twilight renovates my ribcage to stain a loved one on the stems of my spine.
in my windpipe, this nursery of doubt is a nurtured phlegm conceived as a shapeless cloud.
& it pees into my heart & into my brooched navel.

& into my last draft in the clone of a rejection mail.
sorry, this body of commitment isn't quite right for our friendship.
best of luck placing your affection elsewhere.

in the wee hours of a blind moon,
i am a boy camping with a friend's unmentionables in between my collarbones.
his stench do not applaud the wrinkles on my shoulder blade,
or how i untuck the inferno on my wrist.

he fakes his own decamp within my body
& makes a vein stammer at my orphaned silhouette.
i do not document the biometrics of a friend wearing chameleons as a tattoo.
i never fancied rainbows or it's rag of changing colours.

i reached out to my DNA yesterday,
turns out i have a girl's problem.

i celebrate every anniversary with a new guy in my life,
that alone is betrayal enough.

i bake the things i hold dear in my backpack, with no life jacket for toppings.
my body is a cesspool crowded with loved ones hassling over the loose flesh that harbors them.
the universe in a bid to mock me, misplaces the moon in a girl's swimming trunk.

the rest auditions their limbs on a wheelchair,
& urges the Lazarus in me to sponsor her deformities.

-Nnadi Samuel

I am Nnadi Samuel. A 20year old graduate of English & literature from the University of Benin. Have works previously published in libretto magazine, Ace world Publishers, Artifact magazine & a piece titled "My girlfriend says she would die in a street lamp" forthcoming in Jams & Sand magazine. If i am not writing, you find me reading out memes on Facebook @ Samuel Samba.

# Solitude

He said he moved to a bucket inside a cave.

I opened a box that had been closed twenty years

to find sleeping letters written to a remote satellite person.

I tried to welcome, remember her, at least.

Who was this Margaret sending missives from Kodiak, Alaska?

Now was the time to think more deeply of them all:

children of Gaza, trapped in tiny rooms,

beautiful people camped, exhausted, along the Rio Grande,

patting the masa, stirring the beans, on a fire made of sticks

inside a ring of stones, no idea what came next.

Could we ever know how much

had been survived when we had the same house keys

so many years?

*-Naomi Shihab Nye*

Naomi Shihab Nye was born in St. Louis, Missouri. Her father was a Palestinian refugee and her mother an American of German and Swiss descent, and Nye spent her adolescence in both Jerusalem and San Antonio, Texas. She earned her BA from Trinity University in San Antonio. Nye is the recipient of numerous honors and awards for her work, including the Ivan Sandrof Award for Lifetime Achievement from the National Book Critics Circle, the Lavan Award, the Paterson Poetry Prize, the Carity Randall Prize, the Isabella Gardner Poetry Award, the Lee Bennett Hopkins Poetry award, the Robert Creeley Prize, and many Pushcart Prizes. She has received fellowships from the Lannan Foundation, the Guggenheim Foundation, and she was a Witter Bynner Fellow. From 2010 to 2015 she served as a Chancellor of the Academy of American Poets. In 2018 she was awarded the Lon Tinkle Award for Lifetime Achievement from the Texas Institute of Letters. Nye is the Poetry Foundation's Young People's Poet Laureate.

# TAPS

The chilling wind blew through the graveyard
that early December morning
the tombstones standing at attention
as if they were saluting instead of mourning

The sky was a mournful gray
sadness embedded in every cloud
a sea of black suits and dresses engulfed the cemetery
as the sound of twenty-one guns rang out loud

His courage was displayed in red
his purity of ideals in white
and in the sea of blue and stars
you could find his comrades
that fought by his side

As Old Glory was handed to his mother
his commanding officer gave thanks on the country's behalf
his mother heard the words
but her mind and heart was on the soldier
for whom they were playing Taps

-Jose Ponce

Jose M. Ponce has been described as a Chicano Poet, because his poetry reflects the ideals of the Chicano movement in the 1960's, when Latinos started to revolt against the establishment in America. His passion for his culture and the desire to inspire change is clearly found in his poetry

# This Poem Doesn't Exist

Between the thin air and the clouds
only the sun is elemental.
Up here, there are no bones
or breathing lungs
no laments...
only silence.

At the edge of the universe
the twilight
without thorns or petals
takes shelter in the cloud's
shadow
oscillating its luminous veins

across the arterial plough
of its celibate
diaphanous inheritance
where it lays in the subtle
nakedness
of its own smoothness.

Such finesse pale and elusive
under the orphan veil
breaks the knot in an instant
at the sudden sound of the voice,
removing the veil

pouring its sweetness

in the abyss of the earth
at the moment in which
the transparent longitude
destroys the insomnia
crumbling down
when thunder screams.

Without a trace
the wounded clouds spew
their angry drops
on earth's soil nourishing
the flowers, the trees, the worms
and all living creatures.

-*Raúl Sánchez*

Raúl is the newest City of Redmond WA Poet Laureate. He teaches poetry in Spanish at Evergreen High School through the Seattle Arts and Lectures (WITS) program, also at Denny International Middle School through the Jack Straw Educational Project and volunteers for PONGO Teen Writing at the Juvenile Detention Center. He translated Ellen Ziegler's book for the Museum of Antique Mexican Toys. Recently wrote a poem for the Lake City Memorial Triangle, and is working on the Poetic Project "Poetic Trails" for the City of Shoreline.

# Books, Balls, and Candy

I managed to fly from Minnesota
to Florida, getting in after midnight
to be with my mother
in the hospital where she was dying
and after she passed, I spent a week
alone in her condo, going through
everything and getting it ready
to sell and in doing so, I discovered
a drawer full of this and that
and whatnot, the bits and pieces,
the memorabilia of a lifetime
and in that drawer was a lock,
a small vintage Victorian
brass and iron word letter
combination padlock
with pull sideways action,
a padlock with 4 turning barrels
that would spell the password,
READ, which I recalled
quite clearly from my childhood
when my mother told me stories
about how the lock had traveled
from Britain to Australia
and now with her to America
and read was one of the first words
I learned to spell and it's no wonder

really that the first Christmas
when I was old enough to ask
for what I wanted from Santa,
I said I'd like to have books,
balls, and candy

*-Terry Allen*

Terry Allen is an Emeritus Professor of Theatre Arts at the University of Wisconsin-Eau Claire, where he taught acting, directing and playwriting. He is the author of the chapbook Monsters in the Rain (Kelsay Books, 2019). His poems have appeared in many journals, including I-70 Review, Freshwater Poetry Journal, Chariton Review, Third Wednesday, Star 82 Review, Dime Show Review, Popshot Quarterly, Cloudbank, Into the Void and Main Street Rag.

# NURSERY OF WINDS

In the glistening of Spring
young winds are born,
hatchling mouths gaping
for frozen bits of thermal carrion,
gleaning what nourishment they can
from the keening of last winter's gales.

Summertime zephyrs are on their own,
casting themselves in currents of warmth,
deciding from moment to moment
whether they will caress or sting.
They move as they must
for only those most fit
may sail forward into Fall.

Late autumn gales dance in glee,
plucking the trees for adornments
to dress themselves, pushing
the dead scales of summer
through wild ranges
to line west facing cliffs
in hopes of spawning anew.

And in the depths of winter's bite
they prance in waxing and waning strength,
mating with abandon,

showcasing the power of vernal rage,
cradling each other's breezes
in the glacial nooks of high rocks,
Scattering truth in their wake,
waiting for Spring.


-*Christopher Reilley*




Two-time Pushcart nominee Christopher Reilley is a former poet laureate of Dedham, MA, founder of the Dedham Poet Society and the Leicester Writers Guild. He serves on the board of the Worcester County Poetry Association, and his third collection, One Night Stanzas, was recently published by Big Table Publishing.

# Through the Year

Fall is not far
I can hear it in the wind chimes
As September turns to leaves
And cool light
While summer is a fading songbird
And the day is a crow left behind
As I walk in-and-out of the sound
Of crickets
And remember when last winter
Was a snowstorm
And spring was a distant hope.

*-Danny Barbare*

Danny P. Barbare has recently been published in the North Dakota Quarterly and Plainsongs. His poems have been nominated for Best of the Net and have won The Jim Gitting's Award at Greenville Technical College.

# Foreign Service

You can occupy different positions at the same time. In one you are the privileged
child riding the car driven by the driver. In another you are the one with the crooked
legs the others cross the playground to avoid. In one memory someone throws a stone.
It hits you in the cheek and you feel the reverberation of difference. What is it
to be the man with elephantitis who occupies the corner of your street of mansions?
 He lives on a square of cardboard. Sometimes he tilts back his head to admire the play of sunlight in the broad catalpa leaves. The first sketch is loneliness. A series of windows, the glass streaked by clumsy cleaning. A shadow-you behind each one. If you get too close you might shatter. Foreign Service, the name alone implies a sickness. Foreignas in what is not you—and how are you supposed to serve this? In some memories there is gunfire—usually a street away, generally a place you are said to be protected from. And what are they fighting for—the white sliced bread someone serves you on porcelain with frozen rosettes of butter. At times you cannot bear to imagine what you might have become without the crooked legs, which held you in the corners of the room, like a person in a dancing contest who has no hope of ever taking the floor.

-Sheila Black

Sheila Black is the author of four poetry collections, most recently Iron, Ardent (Educe Press, 2017). She is a co-editor of Beauty is a Verb: The New Poetry of Disability (Cinco Puntos Press, 2011). Her poems have appeared in Poetry, The Birmingham Review, The New York Times and other places. She currently divides her time between San Antonio, TX, and Washington, D.C., where she works at AWP.

# Books

Thanks to the woman who threw
books out the window of the library.
Your choice and aim was impeccable.
How did you know to throw out NEGRO
POETRY? I was never the same.

Emerson came next. Grandma's favorite!
So much poetry, old children's books.
I read about magic, fireflies, summer
camp, horseshoe crabs and stoops; girls
who had horses, boys with their secret

gardens. Ever the reader, science
came next. My first book of studies.
I find myself in Sociology, and again, in
Abnormal Psychology and Child Psychiatry.

-Lorna Dee Cervantes

Born in San Francisco, raised in San José, Barrio Horseshoe, Lorna Dee Cervantes was a self-taught activist by 15, an instant mother at 19, taught herself how to run her own printing press and was Founding Editor/Publisher of MANGO Publications at 20, and the author of EMPLUMADA at 24. A XícanIndX poet (Chumash/Purépecha), Cervantes (PhD, History of Consciousness) was a Professor of English for 20 years at CU Boulder, serving as Director of Creative Writing. She identifies as Indigenous American with 5 books in print and writing 5 more in Seattle.

# The Awkward Book

An awkward book sat on the shelf
Alone and untouched for many years
Yet, its gilded pages called to me
Unsure of the weight it carried
I reached for it with cautious hands
Careful not to crack its spine
I lovingly spread it open before me
Delighting in its tight signatures,
I caressed each leaf as if they were
The fingers of a lover's hand
But soon its threads began to fray
Fearful of damaging its frail bindings
I hurriedly placed the awkward book
Back on the shelf were it had sat
I look for it now and then,
But it has somehow been misplaced
Still, I reach for it

-*John Kojak*

John Kojak is a graduate of the University of Texas who now lives and writes in the foothills of Northern California. His short stories and poetry have appeared in numerous publications, including most recently in Pulp Modern, Switchblade, Serial Magazine, The American Journal of Poetry, Harbinger Asylum, and California's Best Emerging Poets 2019.

# CAMPGROUND

A trick shooting priest
palms a canary. Swallows it.
Tents brood gaily on the brown lot.
The sword swallower and
dancing bear swap jokes and recipes.

The circus can't wait
to leave town.

*-Mark Mitchell*

Mark J. Mitchell was born in Chicago and grew up in southern California. His latest poetry collection, Starting from Tu Fu was just published by Encircle Publications.
He is very fond of baseball, Louis Aragon, Miles Davis, Kafka and Dante. He lives in San Francisco with his wife, the activist and documentarian, Joan Juster where he makes his meager living pointing out pretty things. He has published 2 novels and three chapbooks and two full length collections so far. Titles on request. A meager online presence can be found at https://www.facebook.com/MarkJMitchellwriter/

# If you are like me

If you are like me,

You go tango dancing
Rather than watch the Anal Super Bowel

If you are like me,

You have a wild garden
Instead of a manicured lawn

If you are like me,

You shop in family stores
Not in cages that sell everything but harmony

If you are like me,

You like to explore ethnic weird neighborhoods
And escape synthetic suburbs

If you are like me,

You choose your path at your own pace,
Lonely but amazed.

-Carlos Ponce-Melendez

My writings have appeared in Gloom Cupboard, Future Earth, Mississippi Crow, Calliope, Blazevox, Voices Along the River, Small Brushes, among other publications. I'm also the author of a book of short stories in Spanish "Platicas de mi Barrio," Bilingual Press, Arizona State University.

# Class Consciousness

Middle class people tell working class people to laugh at their jokes about taking it easy.

Middle class people tell working class people "if it doesn't scan, it's free."

Middle class people tell working class people to use some of their savings.

Middle class people tell working class people "you should have gone to the doctor sooner."

Middle class people tell working class people to try self-care.

Middle class people tell working class people to watch less TV.

Middle class people tell working class people to move somewhere else.

Middle class people tell working class people, "It's not that expensive."

Middle class people tell working class people to cut back on Starbucks.

Middle class people tell working class people
to get their hands out of their pockets.

Middle class people tell working class people
to leverage their assets.

Middle class people tell working class people,
"Just put it over there. Thanks."

Middle class people tell working class people
to have a nice weekend.

Middle class people tell working class people,
"Let's split the bill."

-*Abigail Carl-Klassen*

Abigail Carl-Klassen is a poet, writer, educator, translator, and activist on the U.S.-Mexico border. She earned her MFA from the University of Texas at El Paso's Bilingual Creative Writing Program. Her book, A'int Country Like You, is available from Digging Press.

# 1 is 2nd

original sidekick showstopper
you are always in second place because
you are too lazy to practice the extra thirty minutes after school
but who bothers practicing when you can get second place without trying

you are good at settling, and
none of this will fucking matter next year anyway

you learned how to lie about where you go at night before you learned how to drive
always in a rush to get nowhere

you're still able to remember the taste of dunk-a-roos when you try hard enough
you want to know the taste of belonging without trying at all

you are still that child who got too far ahead of their parent in the grocery store
anxiety builds a nest and lays eggs in you when you lose sight of your own reflection for five seconds

you still count with your fingers

you still point at the moon when it looks like Kraft Singles, but you're doing it less than before because you hate the number one

either way,
isn't that what life is becoming for you
fewer moments being able to pinpoint what makes you happy

*-Gume Laurel III*

Gume Laurel III is a Texas native, originating from the Rio Grande Valley. Over the past several years, Laurel has dedicated himself to releasing a number of literary works that highlight diverse characters and settings, specifically representative of the Latinx and LGBTQA+ communities. He currently resides in San Antonio, TX and continues to write fictional stories and poetry that is both timely and relevant.

# 45

I'm 45
And my ex-girlfriend
Not even ex-wife
Four days before Christmas
I'm $200 overdrawn
Too broke for food
Orders me a pizza
From 400 miles away

Is that love
Or is that pathetic?
Pathetic of her or me?
   Pathetic
      because I am too fucking busted to feed myself
         or because
            she still love me more than I love myself?

Ex-girlfriend
Not even
Ex-wife
400
Miles away

-PW Covington

PW Covington writes in the beat tradition of the North American highway.
In 2019 his short fiction collection "North Beach and Other Stories" was named a LGBTQ Fiction Finalist by the International Book Awards. Covington lives in Albuquerque, NM. Follow him on Instagram @BeatPW.

# Drive Down 77

I.
A blue barrel waits
Along highway 77.
A tattered white flag
Faded in the sun:
Agua.

II.
Road sign
No citrus plants
beyond this point
.
III.
My image captured.
Who scans the face?
I have no citrus.

IV.
A mile from the Sarita checkpoint:
a maroon lace bra
on the side of the road.
Traffic inches.
My stomach clenches.

V.
Man with dark shades and a menacing dog:

"U.S Citizen?"
"yes."

VI.
Where is the woman who is missing her bra?

*-Samantha Ceballos*

Samantha Ceballos is a Xicana poet studying Literature, Creative Writing, Social Justice at Our Lady of the Lake University in San Antonio. Born in Brownsville and raised in Katy, Samantha explores different social justice topics in her writing, such as women's rights and immigration issues.

# EXPIATION

Motion of Life
Truthward
It is in the tongue
Where
Truth turns untruth
Or the reverse of it
It plays the game of
Cat and mouse

The winner of the game
Is finally found accused
Of hundred sins

So he makes atonement
By setting fire on the face
Of his abode

*-Guna Moran*
*Translated from Assamese - Bibekananda Choudhury*

Guna Moran is an emerging Assamese poet and critic. His poems have been published in various international magazines,- journals and anthologies

# Samaria

Mis ojos a Samaria nunca han visto
ni mis oídos conocen sus cánticos.
Sus vientos no han acariciado mi piel
y sus aromas no me han embriagado.
Sus aguas… ¡Sus aguas nunca he probado!

¿Dónde estás, Samaria? ¿Do tus paisajes?
¿De qué color es tu cielo? ¿Tus campos?
¿Qué forma tienen allí las moradas?
¿Y cómo son tus hondos pozos de agua?

En las noches largas te echo de menos
como si fueras por mí conocida,
como si fueras más que una añoranza.

Te he buscado por miles de caminos
y cuando creo verte, no es más que humo.

Samaria, ¿dónde estás? ¿Existes acaso?

*-Gabriel González Núñez*

Gabriel González Núñez was born in Montevideo, Uruguay, and is currently a Brownsville-based translation professor for UTRGV. He has authored several short stories and poems, which have been published in print and online magazines. He is also the author of several children's books, and the poetry collection "ese golpe de luz" published in January 2020 by FlowerSong Press

# Samaria

Mine eyes have not seen Samaria
and mine ears have not heard her chants.
Her winds have not caressed my skin
and her fragrances have not intoxicated my soul.
Her water... Her water I have never tasted!

Where art thou, Samaria? Where is thy landscape?
What colour are thy heavens? And thy fields?
What is the shape of thy mansions?
And what of thine water wells?
In long nights I pine for thee
as if I knew thee,
as if thou wert more than a longing.

I have sought after thee in a thousand roads,
and when methinks I see thee, it is but smoke.

Samaria, where art thou? Art thou real?

-*Gabriel González Núñez*

Gabriel González Núñez was born in Montevideo, Uruguay, and is currently a Brownsville-based translation professor for UTRGV. He has authored several short stories and poems, which have been published in print and online magazines. He is also the author of several children's books, and the poetry collection "ese golpe de luz" published in January 2020 by FlowerSong Press

# Tragedy And Comedy

Medusa had sex with a bird.
Uranus was impregnated by the sea.
Persephone was seduced by her father
in the form of a serpent.
Pan's flute was once a woman
who rejected his advances.

They were all at it, apparently,
humans restrained in comparison,
tragedy and comedy two sides
of the same cracked and dusty mirror,
the world mad from the hips down.

However much the flesh will eat
the soul is starving.

*-Bruce McRae*


Bruce McRae, a Canadian musician currently residing on Salt Spring Island. BC is a multiple Pushcart nominee with over 1,400 poems published internationally in magazines such as Poetry, Rattle and the North American Review. His books are 'The So-Called Sonnets (Silenced Press); 'An Unbecoming Fit Of Frenzy; (Cawing Crow Press) and 'Like As If" (Pski's Porch), Hearsay (The Poet's Haven).

# A happy young guy

1.
A happy young guy
who smiles for no reason,
a photo from ten years ago

## Unknown

2.
Young and unknown,
except for himself, only mother
knows his name

## Close my eyes

3.
I lie down
and close my eyes,
I see you

-Hadi Panahi


Hadi Panahi is a PhD student of psychology, living in Tehran, Iran. He writes poetry, in particular short poems. His work has been published in Better Than Starbucks (July 2019), Gyroscope Review (Summer-2019), Metafore (Spring 2019), Rigorous (2019, Volume Three, Issue 3) and Dream Catcher (Issue 39).

# Johnny

*"Momma told Johnny not to go downtown, Marine Corps Recruiter was hanging around."*

My son says he wants to be a Marine like me.
A Marine like me.

You're not going to hack it, I say.
You can't even wake up at 6 AM.
There's no urgency in your body.
You're not ready.
Just go to college.
Be an engineer for NASA.

Your Grandma wants you to fight for Trump
and Jesus Christ.
It might settle you down and make a man out of you.
You're not going to make it,
and I'll be damned if you come home on a Greyhound bus.
Dishonorable Discharge forever.

I won't let you down, he says.
Yes, you will.
This isn't the same Corps.
You can try to be an Airman like your bio dad.
There's no way you'll survive the Marines.
You won't even make it past the scale at MEPS.

He pushes his portholes up the bridge of his nose.

His cold stare.

18 years ago,
I picked up the phone,
to hear my uncle say,
I heard you want to be a jarhead.
Mijo, you're not going to make it.
You'll never be able to hack it
I know you and your personality.
You won't make it.
I know I can't stop you.
Stop eating tacos and start working out.
Let me know how it goes.

Yes sir.

One day,
at 2 AM,
while we were sleeping,
Johnny left us,
for a girl,
and Zennial freedom,
whatever that is.

-Vincent Cooper

Vincent Cooper is the author of Where the Reckless Ones Come to Die through Aztlan Libre Press and Zarzamora- Poetry of Survival. Cooper's poems can be found in several zines, journals and anthologies. He is currently working on his memoir and poetry of his time in the Marine Corps Pre/post 9/11.

# The Cost

1.

People say we fell from grace—we fell
walking the path & maybe it's bad
language, philosophy, or faith—truth is we pay
a price we don't decide but we know the cost

Last night, I was humming & singing in my sleep
I remember creaking & rocking steadily in a dream
like a metronome, in the waking world I cried
in the dream—I felt a rough brown hand
on my head & heard a sigh, I am Esteban—

\*


My mouth opened & candies—soft & hard crawled out
—An offering, cried Esteban, we can begin!
Naked but for a filthy loincloth I stood on a wooden
deck, a molded mast, a Portuguese flag stitched into the sail,
& the entire ship in flames yet sailing along
Esteban waved, Come, Mulato, see the first shore:


Tree-dressed mountains, cotton clouds & blue skies—
this island & so many like it—clear waters, pink & black sands
people dancing & drinking dressed like lords & judges,

flags in red & blue, in black & red, yellow & green—
grinding each other to calypso, bachata, soca

Closer—sand choking on shards of beer & tequila bottles—
the bloodied & bare shackled feet of carnival dancers
Hotels shining like pools of water in the hills—a white man posed
on a flat green patch, I thought he waved at us, he was testing
the wind, swung his golf club, wind pressed tee shirt over
his belly—ALL INCLUSIVE in bold black letters

Esteban laughed, a bitter man, The water remembers!
The waters began to rise & rise & rise
The carnival never stopped, shackles & all we dragged
island folk off dry land, & the hotels & white man golfing
blew bubbles & sank to the depths without a sound,
water so clear you could see Middle Passage dead
at the bottom, I know we pay a price we don't decide
but we know the cost
What are my brothers & sisters thinking
as they dance—after all the declarations
of independence—all the independence days
decades pretending white government—
white wigs & all?

& Esteban dragged me by the neck & asked
What do you see there in the water?

2.

You are sixteen & at a pool party The girls are pretty, everyone at the party is Latino, but you know the drill Your own family warned you against dating black people Yet here you are The only black person at the party Latino, yes But black Slowly, less & less "friends" engage you You feel like a guest that's not being asked to leave But you feel like a guest that's no longer wanted The other kids start getting into the pool No one is inviting you No one is acknowledging you Foolishly, you start speaking to people in Spanish You are trying to prove something but no one is listening You are ashamed of your desperation Something somewhere deep inside you is ringing loudly You leave the party and nobody notices A few days later, at school, nobody asks you how you liked the party They talk about it as if you weren't even there As if you hadn't been invited Later you learn about segregation & pools The one drop rule The one black toe in the water rule You learn that DNA is genetic memory—just like water is memory, like survival

3.

My son asks why he's not brown like me

& I think about having the other
talk with him, about passing
& not being able to pass
& don't you even think about passing

Memory takes the moment—I'm running
in the rain with friends
the rain stops against my hair, sits
like cold wax on a wooden table
My afro is not grass laying under water's weight

Your hair's not soft like mine You can't do this

The hand like a buffing pad—makes a shine,
a lacquered lawn I want to torch
      So I slap my friend, in the name
of that narrative:

white is good, black is bad
good hair, bad hair
      You shall not pass

& I tell my son that…

4.

I wanted to wake up—
Esteban gave me a bottle of rum,
They gave us these islands
Little fiefdoms of diaspora, trap—
How long to make slaves into a kingdom again?
Little islands—diaspora of Babel
& the more I drank, the more Esteban cried
& his tongue crawled out of his mouth—a great snake

Give me the bottle
Donne moi la bouteille
Dame la botella
Geef me de fles
I know we pay a price we don't decide
but we know the cost

-*Roberto Carlos Garcia*

Poet, storyteller, and essayist Roberto Carlos Garcia is a self-described "sancocho [...] of provisions from the Harlem Renaissance, the Spanish Poets of 1929, the Black Arts Movement, the Nuyorican School, and the Modernists." Garcia is rigorously interrogative of himself and the world around him, conveying "nakedness of emotion, intent, and experience," and he writes extensively about the Afro-Latinx and Afro-diasporic experience. His second poetry collection, black / Maybe, is available from Willow Books. Roberto's first collection, Melancolía, is available from Červená Barva Press.
He is founder of the cooperative press Get Fresh Books Publishing, A NonProfit Corp.

# The Flight to Johannesburg

We lived together for fourteen hours and three minutes
one industrial nomad, one seeking asylum out of hell
our nuptial contract enforced by silicon chips and
   seating algorithms
we promised nothing
   shared muffins and
   the occasional touch

bad things
   very bad things happened
   she said
her crocodile-skin-shoes went
  tap-tap-tap
her honey-wheat voice rose as the engine revved
camouflaged the night the rebels sprayed their DNA into her

two hundred plus strangers sat around
our nest
   of cheap faux-fur blankets
   and free airline perfume

the metal bird flew on
   over all these stories splattered down below

then as we landed
all her secret sorrows and impossible desires

left her cranium
spilling over my white tee.

*-Partha Mukhopadhyay*

Partha Mukhopadhyay had his first collection of poetry in Bengali, Nachiketar Uttarpatra published in 2014 ( Sopan Publishers. ISBN: 978-93-82433-35-4 ). This work got the best breakout poetry book award in Kolkata. His second collection of original English poetry will be published in 2020.

# MAIN STREET

A sudden dark cloud.
Wait. Only birds.
Headed south, en masse.

It's twilight,
a loose joint in my reasoning.
That's why the sun
is raw material
for my latest fantasy,
poured by me,
sculpted by me.

And nothing to do with the one
that plies its trade
come dawn.

Celia once said that
my eyes don't tell
so very much about me.

Gary likes to point out
that I was wilder in my youth.

Rose reckons that
words fall out of the mouth
like dead Autumn leaves,

although without the colorful history.

Someone's always saying something.

Tonight,
the street lights won't do nearly enough
to protect us from the darkness.
And some will pray.
And others curse.
Both with their heads tilted back,
looking up at God.

By midnight, all will be quiet.
Soon enough, a new day
but the same old Main Street.

-*John Grey*

John Grey is an Australian poet, US resident. Recently published in That, Dalhousie Review and North Dakota Quarterly with work upcoming in Qwerty, Chronogram and failbetter.

# Math

in summation of pandemic outbreak
where a dark government sponsored agent
has altered our biological state
the need for additional provisions
is now a question about life or death

you and a small party head to Zone B
to appropriate medical supplies
to deliver to Zone D in three days
along the way to the very next point
you lose three in a five-biter attack
leaving Zone A you lose another three
as you are surprised by fifteen roamers

you and one other safely reach Zone D
she just bit you… man, this word problem sucks

-Juan Pérez

Juan Manuel Pérez, a Mexican-American poet of indigenous descent and the current Poet Laureate for Corpus Christi, Texas (2019-2020), is the author of WUI: Written Under the Influence of Trinidad Sanchez, Jr. (2011) and Sex, Lies, and Chupacabras (2015), as well as, the co-editor of The Call Of The Chupacabra (2018) and forthcoming Screw The Wall (FlowerSong Press, 2020).

# Amazon

After ten days of raging fire
The calm would descend on the rain forest,
The birds by then had flown away
Braving ashen black sky and suffocating clouds of smoke,
The monkeys , snakes, lemurs, crocs, baboons, zebras, lions and tiger cubs,
They were all too baffled to make out
What happened to their favourite haunts,
orange red flames of fury lighted up the forest like a grand diwali celebration,
Only laughter of hyenas and screams and screeches of animals appeared like a great cacophony,
Were they all celebrating death?
The sooty sky had no answer.

-Moinak Dutta

Born on 5th September, 1977, he has been writing poems and stories from school days. Presently engaged as a teacher of English in a government sponsored institution. Many of his poems and stories are published in national and international anthologies and magazines and also dailies including 'Madras Courier', 'The Statesman' ( kolkata edition), ' World Peace Poetry anthology ' ( United Nations), 'Spillwords' ( published from New York,USA), 'Setu' (published from Pittsburgh, USA,)Riding and Writing ( as a featured poet twice, published from Ohio, USA), ' The Indian Periodical' ' Pangolin Review', ' Tuck Magazine' ' Duane's Poetree', ' Tell me your story' ( literary and travel magazine), ' Nature Writing ' magazine ( U.K.), ' Oddball magazine' 'Soft Cartel' magazine, ' Diff Truths' magazine, ' Ethos Literary Journal',' The Literary Fairy Tales' ' Defiant Dreams' ( a collection of stories on women empowerment published by Readomania, New Delhi ), 'Dynami Zois' ( a selection of short stories comprised of works of authors from India and abroad) ' Muffled Moans' ( a special anthology against women and child abuse, gender violence, published by Authorspress, New Delhi,) etc.

# Budding Romeo
## Ghazal (a poetry form in Hindi & Urdu)

आज हमने यार का घर देख लिया
सच मानो सारा शहर देख लिया

काली चाय ने कुछ ऐसा समां बाँधा
चाँद लम्हों में हमसफ़र देख लिया

उनके गले में चमकते हुए हिरे में
वश में कर लेने वाला पत्थर देख लिया

ऐसा सुकून, ऐसी राहत मिल गयी है
थरथराता अकेलेपन का डर देख लिया

ज़रासी मुस्कानमें हमने कश्ती क्या देखीं
सच मानो सारा समंदर ही देख लिया

## Translation

Today I've visited the home of my beloved.
It seems as if I've visited the entire city.

Black tea created such an atmosphere
I've sensed my partner in just a few moments.

In the shining diamond around her neck
I've seen the stone which hypnotises.

I've felt such a peace and relief
that I've seen the fear of loneliness tremble.

In the slightest of her smiles, I saw a boat.
Trust me, I could visualise the full sea.

*-Jay Gandhi*

Jay Gandhi has been writing poetry since the age of 6. His journey started when he became an active member of the poetry forum poetrycircle.com. Inputs from seasoned poets helped him edit his drafts and slowly he developed his own poetic voice. His Indian background is the spice in his poetry.

# Ave de día

Ave de día quieres ser?
Vuela pues a la luz del sol,
Abre tus alas a los cuatro vientos
Y suelta lo que guardas.

Descúbrele tu pecho al cazador
De mira avariciada,
Y vuela con la cara en alto.

No temas
ni te escondas ante las tormenta.
Con el olivo en el pico,
Vuela con toda tu verdad.

Que la pureza sea tu estandarte.
Cántala en cada árbol
En que posas tu descanso.
Cántasela a la luna de medianoche.

No temas.
No temas al las flechas
Ni a las balas,
Ni a las redes que te tiran.

No temas ave de luz.
Vuela con el sol,

Vuela con la verdad al pico.

*-Alma Quintanilla Castillo*

Alma Quintanilla Castillo is a visual artist and poet in the Rio Grande Valley

# This is all he knows

He drank at home in the backyard; smoking rolled yellowed joints
He smelled forgotten and sad; like old can food and wet books
Staring at nothing, he faced the wall and lost time between sunsets and sunrises

-*Sarai Garcia Martinez*

Sarai has an MA with a focus in English. She writes when she feels like it. Her preference is poetry, but she can dabble in prose. Her writing is small-time local, with no current interest to venture any further. Some of her pieces have been found in previous Boundless editions.

# Awaiting the Heart Attack

Like waiting for labor pains, it's inevitable.
Someday something will boom into my reverie
Of conversation, of gazing at breeze-wafted, sun-gilded leaves,
Of smiling with my purring buddy nestled on my thighs,
Of swinging an eager child, chanting, "Motor boat, motor boat, go so fast!"
Or, "Down, down, baby, down, down the roller coaster!"

Someday comes a knock on the consciousness: a stroke, an attack, a cancer.
Then—should I survive—I'll prudently plan each day,
Forestalling the inevitable.

My children's mourning will indeed come.
But, for now, it's still recess, and no one's at the door.

-*Kathy Trenfield Raines*


Kathy Trenfield Raines has been published in Boundless, Interstice, Escuchame, Voices From the Chicho and Along the River 2. She now writes a bimonthly column for Port Isabel–South Padre Press's Parade insert called, "Creatures Among Us", each article featuring a different animal from the Rio Grande Valley.

# Worn

On any given day I take out the shawl
Constructed from Dad's flannel shirts
Blue plaids and red accents interwoven with
Patterned suspender straps and spats
That brown necktie with white clovers that makes me laugh
Rims of baseball caps stained with sweat
Afghan squares knit by grandmother bordering one edge
Whole sections plagued with the grit of sawdust
Splotches of motor oil and drywall powder, broom straws poking through
Clinging scents of orange rinds and brazil nuts' shells
Fresh cut grass, spaghetti sauce, pancakes
Lineaments and band-aids, burnt toast, newsprint faded and yellow
Hospitals and floor wax, the rubber grips of a cane, then a walker
Settle it around my shoulders like the fragile skin of your hands before the end
Warm and cozy, sometimes heavy, draped like part of me for a few hours, days, weeks
And then I hang it back up for a bit until it's needed once more
Unlike the shawl that was fused by a mesh of brother's crisp white tuxedo shirts
Satin vests and bow ties, black slacks and soft blue jeans worn through to the bones
Quilted jackets and deep v-neck t-shirts in grays and navy
Stitched with guitar strings and backpack straps jangling

carabiner clips
And strips of that ugly-ass blanket from his early twenties
Edges reeking of tobacco and incense, Bvlgari cologne, high-end Italian fare
And greasy take-out, burritos and burgers
A splash of Grand Maranier, cheap wine
Dotted with pockets holding travel sanitizer, USB's, dude wipes, and two-dollar bills
Wrapped tightly on the surface of my skin like a wetsuit of armor
Every hour, day, week, moment since that phone call
Shielding against the shocking surreality and burden that's too raw and bloody to face
Naked

*-Elizabeth S. Hollenbeck*

Elizabeth Hollenbeck is a librarian by profession, writer by calling, and artist through and through. She writes poetry and fiction, and is one of the founders of the McAllen Public Library Writing Circle. She is currently working on her first novel manuscript.

# I Write to Extract

I scratch and pick
through the textured
scar tissue on my chest
tearing away
layer after layer
till the skin
is thin enough to pierce

The flesh sighs
as it splits open
weeping warm fluid

I push deep
tunnel through the chunks
now slick from the gush
My fingers slosh around
till I find it

The calcified mass
Is webbed with
thick muscle strands
I claw and yank
snapping the cords

Scoop out the mass
from the mushy

rotting meat
like pitting an over ripened peach
My chest heaves with relief

Fingers dripping red ink
I place them on a crisp
white sheet
and write

*-Santa Ramirez*

Santa Martinez Ramirez resides in McAllen, Texas. She earned her MA in English, with a certificate in Mexican American studies, at UTRGV in 2019. Her work is featured in UTRGV's The Gallery (2012, 2014, 2017, 2019), and Windward Review. She has been performing her poetry in the RGV since 2012.

# Beatitudes for the Hideous

Blessed are they who don't recoil in horror or gape at their shape
Blessed are they who see their true worth
And don't think they should have been put down at birth
Blessed are they not impulsive automatically seeing them as repulsive?
Blessed are they who don't play the fool reacting with ridicule
Blessed are the good that see them as flesh and blood
Blessed are they who don't deride but think of the person inside
Blessed are they who tarry a while in the hope of seeing them smile
Blessed are those who see them as whole
For they have looked into their eyes and seen the beauty of their soul

*Dedicated to Sarah, a young woman I supported as a care worker and in whom when she smiled at me I saw in her eyes a beauty no artist or photographer could capture.

-Trev Wainwright

Also known as Trev the Road Poet and The Rhymey Limey, Trev is one of Yorkshire's most prolific poetry exports to Texas. Seemingly able to catch a moment in time and put it in rhyme, he is a regular and popular performer at the RGVIPF liked by many.

# El peligro de la noche violada

Todos los cantos han conocido tu voz
palabra del pecho generado
en vidas tatuadas de placer

eres el peligro de la noche violada
la tortura de la esquina escondida
el sentimiento de las lápidas contempladas

con tanta furia enredada de subsuelos sexuales
con tantos ecos rojos perforados

en mañanas de silencios y éxtasis
en noches de sudores y llantos
en tardes de cuevas encendidas

por esta amenazada furia de amor
por este homicidio de la fuerza entregada
por lo causante que queda repetido

desde esta parte de lo deshecho
desde el contorno de lo amamantado
desde este rendimiento que no espera

a esta voz que se ahoga en el pecho
a este tacto del dolor que conoce

los plomos encadenados
las trenzas de los cuerpos arropados

para no sentir el regreso
para quedarse en la espera

del minuto en torbellinos
porque ha sido la muerte
de la piel
la vida
del homicidio en el amor

-Benito Pastoriza Iyodo

Benito Pastoriza Iyodo is a poet residing in McAllen, TX. He writes about sexuality, social-political issues, and history. His published books are: Brothel of the word, A matter of men, September elegies, Waters of paradise, Letters to the shadow of your skin, Beloved, beloved of my heart. He has won numerous literary awards and his works are included in anthologies in various countries.

# Country Nights

I still see your Black Crowes t-shirt hanging off your left shoulder
and me- clinging right onto your every word
you got magenta lipstick on my blunt-
and me- I fell even further and further into you
Your memory is the best part of my history
sweatin' in the Virginian rain
me on you, you on me
reverse and repeat
I still recall that Wyoming night we went to freeze
I tucked you into like 20 blankets and put the janky space heater on your side
finally, you fell asleep and I turned to keep watch over the stars
until all them neon lights went to sleep one by one across all the bars
Honestly, your memory is the best part of me
reminds me of when I was free, I mean really free
Even now, the taste of lipstick + tequila reminds me of you leavin' me
I know it was best for you, sometimes, I just wish it would have been good for me
I'm still walking in the Virginia rains
chasing beers chasing shots chasing trains
You said you were off to Portland
I shoulda asked you- Oregon or Maine?

-*Christian Garduno*

Christian Garduno lives and writes along the South Texas coast, balancing between Forensic Files and Moscow Mules.

# The Winter

My thoughts are laying
Still frozen in the ark
Which are floating
On the velvet of the dark.

A saffron leaf glides
On the snow gleaming
Reaches the earth
Of heaven, dreaming.

A weary tree hangs
Sparkles on its tips
Winter overtakes and
Summer slowly slips.

-Dr.Tejaswini Patil, Maharashtra, India

Dr. Tejaswini Patil is an academician, poet and social worker; writes about Nature, social issues, feminist sensibilities and her experiences. Her books include, 'Talons and Nets', 'Verses of Silence', 'A Glass of Time' and 'Kaainat'. Part of the famous Coffee Table Book, 25 Women of Virtue. Awarded with 'Master of Creative Impulse' by World Poetry Conference, Punjab.

# Desert Lament

Does the water still flow in the acequia,
Rising from burbling springs at the base of the mountain,
Thrumming its way past broken-down apple trees,
Wild plums and sweet pears?
Down
Down
Down
Past the tall spiked tules,
Into the fields of hay and alfalfa,
Seeping into the roots of ancient cottonwoods,
Delivering sweet wetness to the roses by the mission.
Does the water still flow in the acequia?
Does God still dwell in the valley?
Tell Me.

-LuLynne Streeter

LuLynne Streeter is an award-winning author, poet, journalist and 2017 Pushcart Prize nominee and 2015 recipient of the Christina Sergeyevna Prize at the Austin International Poetry Festival. Publication credits include San Pedro River Review, Vagabonds: Anthology of the Mad Ones, Di-Verse-City, and Boundless.

# The Great American Windmill Bob Kaufman Destroyed

Not Wilhelmina's, south past the brewhaus
wordhoard hacked away
Rimbaud stigmata pierced
stoned, giant's maimed roar
forever bellows—Tokáy bottle
shatters silence to spew
like wino in cell

armless giant
splinter by splinter
eyes
the surf
hurl—
All Those Ships
3

Bob Kaufman would sleep
windmill arms, so
would bark at Cafe Babar
he was resting in the
that he slayed
thug in a flood.
cab backseat, Bob
a cross

on broken slats
Jack Micheline
he said,
giant's arms
snug as a
In Harold Norse's
died holding
voodoo menorah

*-Tom Murphy*

Tom Murphy's books are: Pearl (Flower Song Press 2020), American History (Slough Press, 2017), co-edited Stone Renga (Tail Feather, 2017), chapbook, Horizon to Horizon (Strike Syndicate, 2015). Murphy is Langdon Review's 2020 Writer-In-Residence. Murphy is a committee member of the People's Poetry Festival of Corpus Christi.

# A Little Less Sad

I gave birth to you in a parking lot
I just started talking to my phone
so she could write my poems, the other day
I was in the parking lot of Snowball Express
thinking of buying a combo loko
of elote con chile in a cup,
a chamoyada loka and a pingüino split,
for six dollars because I don't know about you
but food always makes me feel good
como dicen "las penas con pan son menos"
but I was so sad and frustrated
that instead, I starting thinking of a poem
so she wrote "I would input you,"
she did not know Spanish
so I decided to speak in English
so she could make sense of herself
and my poem title ended up being "Time"
instead of the longer version in Spanish,
because everything in Spanish is longer, instead of "Tiempo te odio,"
so I will read you the English version
because I haven't had time today to translate to Spanish
which will end up being longer anyways
and heavier and more sentimental
and yes, I left the parking lot empty handed
but with a poem in my phone

that made the rain stop, that made me feel a little less sad,
a little lighter, thinking of the promise
of frijoles a la charra at my mom's house for free
who is always eager to listen to me
speak in my native tongue.

*-Erika Elisa Garza Tamez*

Erika Elisa Garza Tamez is originally from Cd. Mier, Tamaulipas, México. She holds a Master's Degree of Arts in Spanish from UTPA. Garza is currently a Spanish Dual Instructor at La Joya Early College High School. Her poems have been published in the FEIPOL Anthology 2018 Edition and Boundless 2019.

# Isabel

what was your favorite color
what was your go-to karaoke song
how old were you when you first dyed your hair
when did you know you were an artist
when did you know you were a feminist
when did you know you were an angel
one that would fly over the dreams of your loved ones
one that knew how to adorn walls with your light
your laughter permeate with the morning dew

Isabel

whom paints my face with tears today
I would like to offer you an apology
for choosing silence whenever I heard a sexist remark
for swallowing my pain instead of spitting it out because
I thought suffering was synonymous with woman

Isabel

though we never met
I recognize our struggles are one and the same
I just hope that wherever you are now
you adorn and paint
your hair
your nails

your lips
all the colors you love
and you let us take care of the rest
so when you hear our solidarity chants
you may feel our embrace

*-Anatalia Vallez*

Anatalia Vallez is a writer, performer, artivist passionate about using art as a tool for creating consciousness and community. Addressing everything from migration, machismo and our relationship to nature, she seeks to find intimate truths and plant seeds to change the world. First published in Barrio Writers at seventeen, she's taken writing workshops with Las Dos Brujas, Winter Tangerine, Breath of Fire Latina Theater Ensemble and through CREAR Studio's DIY MFA program. Her first book of poetry and monologues: the most spectacular mistake (FlowerSong Press) is forthcoming in April 2020. To find out more visit: anataliavallez.com

# Academic Award For the Movie, "Ars Poetica"

Dreamt one of my poems became a movie and I played the poet character and got an Academy award for Best Actress and in my acceptance speech I began "Thank you" before listing all of the names of poets coming to me and I went on and they went on and no one could get me off the stage and the world started to die with heretofore alien viruses sucking up the air and mountains imploding from within to lay atop smoldering valleys as both awaited the plastic-flecked water of rising oceans and reddened eyes kept popping out from the faces of gowned- and tuxedoed-humans in front of me but I kept talking and naming and naming and naming the poets in a speech whose list began with the most famous poet in human history--"Anonymous"--and continued so that when the universe died the last word uttered was of and by a poet

-Eileen R. Tabios

Eileen R. Tabios has released about 60 collections of poetry, fiction, essays, and experimental biographies from publishers in ten countries and cyberspace. Most recently, she released a short story collection, PAGPAG: The Dictator's Aftermath in the Diaspora and a poetry collection, The In(ter)vention of the Hay(na)ku: Selected Tercets 1996-2019. The inventor of the hay(na)ku, a 21st century diasporic poetic form, she has seen her writing and editing works receive recognition through awards, grants and residencies. More information is available at http://eileenrtabios.com

# Claremont Avenue

We lived there, under the overpass, above the bakery
where they made the thin cookies sticky with molasses
and raisins, beside the all-night convenience store
where they sold wax roses in thin glass tubes,
sealed on both ends with a coating of lipstick-pink wax,
and the roses were tossed away, and the glass
tubes used as crack pipes, which was why they sold them.

Lynne said it was like being in a blood stream—the girders
filigreeing our faces, our bodies humming
with subterranean urgency. You have heard the violence;
I will sing you instead the tenderness between us,
such raucous and sluiced heavens that could turn even hell
into a familiar spirit. Bagels and their moist yeasty
smell, the stray dogs that used to rest with Lynne and I
at the bus stop before dawn when we needed to go
fetch Will from New Jersey—pay his bail, or his music
manager, always some angry man on the other end of the line,
shouting because he had learned threats work like fists.

Above, a plane flies into the future. Our ideas
of romance become obsolete—even so I picture us,
lingering, want to believe Lynne held the world in her
blue hands—the spoon, the match, the way the most imperfect
part of yourself is also the most creative—or so I read
today in O Magazine. But that plane with its plume of

trailing smoke tells another story. What other world might we have made? This ecology of damage—it is all I know; the dear dawn hour when the corner bakery opened its steel doors with a shudder and all we wanted was something sweet.

-Sheila Black

Sheila Black is the author of four poetry collections, most recently Iron, Ardent (Educe Press, 2017). She is a co-editor of Beauty is a Verb: The New Poetry of Disability (Cinco Puntos Press, 2011). Her poems have appeared in Poetry, The Birmingham Review, The New York Times and other places. She currently divides her time between San Antonio, TX, and Washington, D.C., where she works at AWP.

# Traficante

Because I am a smuggler
soy traficante, I deal in
illicit phraseology, I speak
in illegal tongues
I trade in mad metaphors
recently released from
straightjacket stifling.
I revel in forgotten
memory colored with
ancient glyphs and told
to me by candle-light
under cover of night
by sage poets and
truthtellers too many
are too blind or too vain
to recognize or uncover
Good morning boys and
girls, can you say Burciaga
or Anaya or Anzaldua?
If they're banning me in
Arizona it's because we're
banned from the beginning
Even baby Brown Berets
in East LA are bereft and
have been denied a
birthright writ in the blood

of prison poets like Salinas,
Sanchez and Jimmy Baca
We are born smugglers
of la palabra, predisposed
to papyrus and now grown
numb in front of television
fiction. Malverde smiles on
us nonetheless. Porque
somos traficantes y mi vicio
siempre será la letra de la
libertad, la metáfora
desencadenada de un
pueblo equipado, armed
with untold  history and the
books they try to take, we
are the inevitable song and
lyric they will try to silence,
unable to put aside their fear
and hate, dressing it in a
need to enforce the nation's
laws and protect the borders
imposed at the barrel of a gun.
But bullets will never stop the
stampede of lyrical truth or the
blessing of a barrio bard who
took me under wing to show me
words were sacred like the sweat,
that true traficantes know routes
from underground presses to

university halls like the backs of
their tattooed hands, and we
will slang prose and poetry,
newsprint and blog until they
finally and truly reveal themselves
for the fascist, book burners they
are and will always be, knowing
deep down in their true souls that
despite Manifest Destiny, this land
is not theirs and never was.
Soy traficante orgulloso en idiomas
y sonetos, en el olor de la canción
y el canto de las flores, soy voz
y luna como baile entre mi madre
y el futuro de la tierra maya quiche
I traffic in banned books and
felonious turns of phrase, because
this is all I know.

-*Abel Salas*

Based in Los Angeles, journalist and poet Abel Salas has written for The Austin Chronicle, Los Angeles Times Magazine, Los Angeles Magazine, LA Weekly and the New York Times, among others. His poems have appeared in Zyzzyva, Beltway Quarterly, Cutthroat: A Journal of the Arts, Cipactli and Huizache, Americas Review as well as the anthologies Poetry of Resistance: Voices for Social Change (University of Arizona Press, 2016) and The Coiled Serpent: Poets Arising From the Cultural Quakes and Shifts of Los Angeles (Tia Chucha Press, 2016). Internationally, his poems have appeared in the anthology Huellas a Través del Tiempo (Ajalpan, Pueblam SIPEA, 2014) and in the regional edition of Mexico's second largest national daily La Jornada (Zacatecas, Zacatecas) He is the editor and publisher of Brooklyn & Boyle, a community, arts and cultural monthly and was a co-founder of Corazón del Pueblo, a grass-roots arts, education and political action center in Boyle Heights.

## Ode to an Avocado

You!

Shaped like an ovum seed in the middle
of the branches hanging with all your brothers
and, perhaps your sisters.

Did you know that I've known you since I was five?
I really didn't   really   know   you    then
but I heard about you at that time.

You were presented, introduced in my mouth
as a mushy-soft, sometimes tangy-spicy-oniony-decadent
delicacy served in small bowls and dipping dishes.

That soft green creamy buttery meat
sensation in my palate could not
identify the deliciousness under

the hard crusty skin that protects you.
Dark green as my midnight dreams, bumpy
as the cloudy days bereft of sun-light

Where have you been? Oh, I see, hiding beneath
the bushel crates of transported, imported food
other immigrants harvested at the right time

south of the equator where alpacas, mules, donkeys
and mountain goats go. Handled by those humble
brown skinned hands from faraway lands

where the sun shines brighter.
You are free! But trapped
in a plastic mesh

with five other guys
your friends I presume, even though
the sign says 4 in a pack.

Ahuacatl, is your name!
but nobody calls you that
I think I know why

-Raúl Sánchez



Raúl is the newest City of Redmond WA Poet Laureate. He teaches poetry in Spanish at Evergreen High School through the Seattle Arts and Lectures (WITS) program, also at Denny International Middle School through the Jack Straw Educational Project and volunteers for PONGO Teen Writing at the Juvenile Detention Center. He translated Ellen Ziegler's book for the Museum of Antique Mexican Toys. Recently wrote a poem for the Lake City Memorial Triangle, and is working on the Poetic Project "Poetic Trails" for the City of Shoreline.

# Bowie's Lazarus

I'll be free
it's time...my life has burst
exploded a million shades
of burnt ochre and crimson tides
charred and bleeding still

the blood in my veins
flow, Goya and a tinge
cruel, the strikes of English red
and the whiff of blue velvet grips

in a blaze of burnt carmine
ripples of claret and faded roses
long forgotten my fiery dreams arise
in wisps of morphine for my pain

it is time for the last of the blues
chants of long forgotten madrigal
drops of bittersweet memories
so long music...it is time

© *Sandhya Suri*

*About this piece -*
*David Bowie passed away in January of 2016. I grew up listening to his music. Scrap books were filled with picture cut outs of him. I will never forget Labyrinth. To me, that film stayed in my memory. When he passed away, I wrote this piece that was dedicated to him. This one is for Bowie.*

Sandhya Suri is an Indian Navy Veteran who is now a Change Enabler and professional speaker. Her first co-authored political fiction will be out in June. She is an established poet and is now working on her second book which is about her life's experiential journey. Her belief system is a blend of ikigai, kintsugi and meraki. She currently lives in Delhi, India.

# Chorizaso

*for my wife*

you are like unexpected chorizo
flavorful, spicy, and so full of life
inside your warm, soft tortilla blanket
what a morning surprise for both of us

-*Juan Perez*

Juan Manuel Pérez, a Mexican-American poet of indigenous descent and the current Poet Laureate for Corpus Christi, Texas (2019-2020), is the author of WUI: Written Under the Influence of Trinidad Sanchez, Jr. (2011) and Sex, Lies, and Chupacabras (2015), as well as, the co-editor of The Call Of The Chupacabra (2018) and forthcoming Screw The Wall (FlowerSong Press, 2020).

# Release It

I want to live in the bedroom tunes played for me on your guitar
I want to live in our highs and cancel our lows
I want to discard all of the words you calculate carefully to execute the lowest blow
I want to live in your hands pinning mine down
I want to exist in the journal I gifted you but have never been let into
I want to drown out the sound of you slut shaming me
I want to erase all former lovers
Letter by letter until its only your name on the chalkboard
I want to hold the feeling
Cradle it
Release it
And know we made the right decision
I want to be reassured by you
Not always but every so often
I want to scribble it on the walls
I want to shout it
I want to live in those first few months
I want to position it
Wedged between sunset and sundown
I want to be the hair tucked behind each other's ears
I want the manic-
The empathetic-
The "I'm driving you to drink" statements
I want you to believe that I am sick-to-my-stomach sorry

I want to erase every ounce of resentment
I want to be the first person you think to call
When you need to be talked down from jumping
I want you
More than I've ever longed for anything
I want to stop pretending that I'm ok
And actually feel ok
And I want to release the breath I've been holding

*-Briana Muñoz*

Briana Muñoz is the author of "Loose Lips", a poetry collection published by Prickly Pear Publishing. More of her works have been published in the Bravura Literary Journal, LA BLOGA, an online publication, and in the Oakland Arts Review and the St. Sucia zine. When she isn't typing away, she enjoys traveling, live music, cats, and thrift stores.

# Abused in the rain

Like a neglected dog
tied up outside a bookshop in the rain
even a bicycle
would tell you it's had enough
if it could after a while.

-*Andy N*

Andy N is a writer, performer, podcaster, creative writing workshop tutor and sometimes experimental musician from Manchester who also currently co running Stretford's always welcoming spoken word night 'Speak easy' and has published three full length poetry collections, the most recent been 'Birth of Autumn' He is the creator / editor of 'Spoken Label', which since 2016 has done over 120 Podcasts with a whole host of writers, artists etc and with his partner co runs the review Podcast series 'Reading in Bed' and assists with the running of 'Printed Words'. He also does ambient music under the name of Ocean in a Bottle.

His official website is: http://onewriterandhispc.blogspot.co.uk/

# Niña sin nombre

Golpe certero
en el pecho

una víctima más,
niña sin nombre.

¡Hijas arrebatadas
de los caminos!

Gimes en la
penumbra

por el abuso
de tu cuerpo.

Niña sin nombre
en las calles adoquinadas.

La inocencia
fue lluvia.

Tu carne lacerada
por el viento.

Tus entrañas
desgarradas.

¿Quién impide hacerte justicia?
¿Quién impide tu curación?

Se escurren las
silenciosas lágrimas
de sangre.

Se desbordan
los ríos
color carmín.

¡Cubren las calles!

¡Cuántas anónimas voces!

-Xánath Caraza

Xánath Caraza is a traveler, educator, poet, short story writer, and translator. She writes for La Bloga, The Smithsonian Latino Center, Revista Literaria Monolito, and Seattle Escribe. In 2019 for the International Latino Book Awards she received Second Place for Hudson for "Best Book of Poetry in Spanish" and Second Place for Metztli for Best Short Story Collection. In 2018 for the International Latino Book Awards she received First Place for Lágrima roja for "Best Book of Poetry in Spanish by One Author" and First Place for Sin preámbulos / Without Preamble for "Best Book of Bilingual Poetry by One Author". Her book of poetry Syllables of Wind / Sílabas de viento received the 2015 International Book Award for Poetry. She was Writer-in-Residence at Westchester Community College, NY, 2016-2019. Caraza was the recipient of the 2014 Beca Nebrija para Creadores, Universidad de Alcalá de Henares in Spain. She was named number one of the 2013 Top Ten Latino Authors by LatinoStories.com. Her books of verse Where the Light is Violet, Black Ink, Ocelocíhuatl, Conjuro and her book of short fiction What the Tide Brings have won national and international recognition. Her other books of poetry are It Pierces the Skin, Balamkú, Fără preambul, Μαύρη μελάνη, Le sillabe del vento, Noche de colibríes, and Corazón pintado. Caraza has been translated into English, Italian, Romanian, and Greek; and partially translated into Nahuatl, Portuguese, Hindi, and Turkish.

# Girl with No Name

Direct blow
to the chest

one more victim,
girl with no name.

Daughters snatched
off the streets!

You moan in
the shadows

your body
abused.

Girl with no name
on cobblestoned corners.

Innocence
became rain.

Your flesh slashed
by wind.

Your entrails
torn asunder.

Who stops justice?
Who stops your healing?

Silent tears
of blood
seeping down.

Carmine colored
rivers
slip their banks.

They fill the streets!

So many anonymous voices!

-Xánath Caraza, translated by Sandra Kingery

Xánath Caraza is a traveler, educator, poet, short story writer, and translator. She writes for La Bloga, The Smithsonian Latino Center, Revista Literaria Monolito, and Seattle Escribe. In 2019 for the International Latino Book Awards she received Second Place for Hudson for "Best Book of Poetry in Spanish" and Second Place for Metztli for Best Short Story Collection. In 2018 for the International Latino Book Awards she received First Place for Lágrima roja for "Best Book of Poetry in Spanish by One Author" and First Place for Sin preámbulos / Without Preamble for "Best Book of Bilingual Poetry by One Author". Her book of poetry Syllables of Wind / Sílabas de viento received the 2015 International Book Award for Poetry. She was Writer-in-Residence at Westchester Community College, NY, 2016-2019. Caraza was the recipient of the 2014 Beca Nebrija para Creadores, Universidad de Alcalá de Henares in Spain. She was named number one of the 2013 Top Ten Latino Authors by LatinoStories.com. Her books of verse Where the Light is Violet, Black Ink, Ocelocíhuatl, Conjuro and her book of short fiction What the Tide Brings have won national and international recognition. Her other books of poetry are It Pierces the Skin, Balamkú, Fără preambul, Μαύρη μελάνη, Le sillabe del vento, Noche de colibríes, and Corazón pintado. Caraza has been translated into English, Italian, Romanian, and Greek; and partially translated into Nahuatl, Portuguese, Hindi, and Turkish.

# The willows

The willows sway along the river
      step into shallows with open arms
            and whisper from time to time.
A measured humming hovers in the breeze
      while pateros drift across the sleeping serpent
            pushing hidden shadows off the carrizales.
A flock of house sparrows pierces the obsidian night
      chasing feeding fields on the other side.
Camouflaged harriers perched on mezquites
      pounce on them at first strands of light.
Tangled in fear, a handful scuffle away,
      feathers flutter on the spines of nopaleras.
The day bleeds beyond the sunrise
      and alas blancas echo another song.
Startled, the willows shudder
      the river scurries downstream
            the wind scrambles away.
Peregrines drift the free-flowing skies.
      Coyotes crack the stone-cold silence.
All wait…wait…wait…for another day.

-*Javier Villareal*

Javier Villarreal holds a BA and MA in Spanish from Pan American University, Edinburg, Texas, and a PhD in Hispanic Linguistics from The University of Texas at Austin, Texas. His major fields of interests are Languages in Contact (Spanish and English), Mexican American Folklore, and Creative Writing. His works have been published by academic, literary journals, and anthologies. His first book of poetry Entre lluvia, canto y flor was published in 2008. He translated Versos para no dormir (Leticia Sandoval), edited Voz de Amor (Servando Cárdenas), and is currently working on his second book of poetry, and other projects. After 30 years in academia, and the last 24 at Texas A&M University-Corpus Christi, Javier has retired. He resides in Corpus Christi with his family and writes and promotes cultural events in South Texas.

# December 3rd, 2007

At three pounds and fourteen ounces
You shook the world
Fists like lightning bolts
Tiny hands holding tight
Fingers round my thumb

And I want you to know
You were too small to carry home
Premature and incubated
So we waited a cold thirty-eight days
Through Christmas and New Years

Toughest baby I'd ever known
So alone during nights
Baby wrists and baby ankles
Pricked and pieced
But baby girl you pulled through

And I want you to remember
You were born with flames
Blazing round your soul
Coal on the path of life
So light it up – WildFire

You're like the wild flowers
Persistent and resistant

Merry meadows – grow – you gotta go
Burn hues, my child, with the petals
Of your dancing daisy smile

-*Mark Esperanza*

Mark Esperanza is an Edcouch-Elsa writer who currently teaches at Progreso High School and Northwest Vista College. He resides in Edinburg, TX with his family and is committed to the next step of his writing career: publications.

# Thirty Something

father sings amazing grace in church
does not know the son is lost
finding the hands on the clock are hooves
bouldering forward
elegant tap dances
humble last bets
son mimicking the lyrics of father's ancient lips so to
make him proud
but time is running out
in this round, time is running short
replicated behaviors unmasking themselves to be continued
trauma
down the hatch it goes
turning thirty something happens too fast
hard to keep up
rowing faster
out of breath
a new day is supposed to come, but who knows when we'll see it
turning thirty something takes so damn long
encouraged to know i'll get to where i'm going if i try hard
enough
down every road, until what's lost has been found

-*Gume Laurel III*

Gume Laurel III is a Texas native, originating from the Rio Grande Valley. Over the past several years, Laurel has dedicated himself to releasing a number of literary works that highlight diverse characters and settings, specifically representative of the Latinx and LGBTQA+ communities. He currently resides in San Antonio, TX and continues to write fictional stories and poetry that is both timely and relevant.

# The lost leaf

When the pink leaf comes out from the soft window of a branch, it doesn't know that the limited scope of its exaltation is also predetermined. We notice changes in its color, shape, and luster along with the change of weather.

Its own branches throw it on the ground where it transforms into pale and seems like lifeless. The wind wishes to blow the leaf in a moment. Before the leaf can understand something, it finds itself flowing in the cool water.

Waves want to reconcile its sorrows and pain in itself, but its dilapidated existence has become weightless. Now it can fly, can flow away but can't drown.

The edges too want to touch the leaf but are afraid of the waves. The waves also don't want to harm the leaves by its rude conduct. Finally, waves transfer the leaf to the edges. Though the edges are emotional yet they don't want to challenge the laws of nature.

On the threshold of the shores, the leaf ultimately ensures its courage to be transformed into an incorporeal shape. These struggles have left no shortcoming to make it colorless and unmistakable. Slowly, it has converted into completely porous in shape, but in this new form, the best shape engraved by the naturalistic artwork is created!

It's a strange custom of the world! A time, the leaf that was separated by its own branch has found shelter in the soft pages of the book that has given it a new identification of co-ownership!

Even today, that leaf has emerged from the brutal cycle of death and has become a silent, firm and an immense source of inspiration among people!

-*Durgesh Verma*

Durgesh Verma is a Social Worker in Uttar Pradesh, India. 7 of his compositions are published in USA in Feelings International: A Book of International Artists Vol.2, 3 of his compositions are published in Canada in Voices of Humanity Volume 2 and a composition is published in Australia in THE AUSTRALIA TIMES POETRY- Volume 4 No.23. A University post graduate, Durgesh post graduated with a degree in Commerce from Mahatma Gandhi Kashi Vidyapeeth University, Varanasi. In his spare time he enjoys listening to all genres of music, swimming, writing poems in Hindi, Urdu & English, which may help lead to global peace and harmony.

# I am not ashamed

Come, Child,
Put your hands in mine.
I'll take you to the land of fairies.
Don't feel ashamed
For your soiled hands…
I am not…

This way, dear,
This is the way to Truth.
There are many deceptive turns
Leading to foil and burns…
You might have turned on one …
Take the right path anew.
Don't feel ashamed of
walking on wrong roads…
I am not…

-Dr.Tejaswini Patil, Maharashtra, India


Dr. Tejaswini Patil is an academician, poet and social worker; writes about Nature, social issues, feminist sensibilities and her experiences. Her books include, 'Talons and Nets', 'Verses of Silence', 'A Glass of Time' and 'Kaainat'. Part of the famous Coffee Table Book, 25 Women of Virtue. Awarded with 'Master of Creative Impulse' by World Poetry Conference, Punjab.

# Before Work

Dainty cherry tomatoes,
Bits of spinach delicately
Sauteed in extra virgin olive oil,
Brighten my morning frittata.

Many breakfasts removed from
Platters of scarlet tomato slices,
Biscuits and eggs fried with bacon.
My grandmother's morning fare.

She and her brothers sold
Fruit and vegetables from
Pickup trucks parked
Alongside the road.

Tomatoes were their specialty.
Rising before dawn, she
Packed the small baskets with
Red-ripened jewels.

Sometimes I went with her.
She whistled to the radio.
Bought me lunch and,
Talked about when I grew up.

It's the tomatoes.

They bring her back to me.
Like that second cup of coffee
Before I sit at my desk and dream.

*-LuLynne Streeter*

LuLynne Streeter is an award-winning author, poet, journalist and 2017 Pushcart Prize nominee and 2015 recipient of the Christina Sergeyevna Prize at the Austin International Poetry Festival. Publication credits include San Pedro River Review, Vagabonds: Anthology of the Mad Ones, Di-Verse-City, and Boundless.

# Wick Work

The thirsty wick drinks from its mother's match.

Wax drips from its extended, yellow-green flame,
trembling in the shadow of its own candle.

Like invisible hands clapping,
eddies of air alternately fuel and cool.
The beam burns and bejewels forming a flowing harness of pearls.

Erratically, the flame flickers,
its black tongue drools with melt.
Pools of hot spit spill over thin, radial gums.
Down over what was once white, smooth and tapered.

A life-form grows out of the struggle:
heat versus light, round versus randomness, grace against gravity.
Swollen appendages sag in place:
jaws, lobes, hips, jowls
toes with brows, nose upon knees.

Shorter now with considerable girth, she cannot breathe;
she chokes on wax-flow in an effort to swallow her fat faster than it forms.
At wick's end, she is exhausted…

A micro-dune of char dismembered by a gust of wind,
her last light breaks up into a million grains filtered down to a spark.

Then dark.

*-Judith P. Oppenheim*

Judith P. Oppenheim is a new poet having discovered the Friendswood Poets Workshop in 2018. Her ekphrastic work Moran Transported received Honorable Mention at their 2019 Fall Festival. With imagery and anthropomorphism, she engages the reader in a world where every object is alive with feelings.

## A Purple Cow

I wish I had a Purple Cow.
It's such a lovely hue.
I wonder if the chocolate milk
Would come out purple too!

## A Tabby Cat

I wish I had a tabby cat.
He'd prob'ly eat my Skittles.
Indubitably fat,
He'd eat my doggy's vittles.

## A Yellow Rat

I wish I had a fat yellow rat.
I'd name him Butter—or maybe Pat.

I'd feed him bananas!
And American cheese!
So he'd stay super yellow—
But fuzzy—like bees!

His paws would be black—though
I'd paint his claws neon—so they could glow.
That might sound kinda silly, but it's not a lark:
I could easily track him—even in the dark—
If he ever got loose at night from his cage!
(I could never do that if he was grey or beige.)

-*Daniel García Ordaz*

TEDx Speaker Daniel García Ordaz, a.k.a. The Poet Mariachi, a teacher at La Joya Early College High School, is an established voice in Mexican American poetry. His work has been taught and written about by academics across the U.S. and abroad and he is a 2018 Pushcart Prize nominee. García has an MFA in Creative Writing from UTRGV.

## Losing Sight

I remember the spring warblers
perched on a red cedar rail
outside my kitchen window. Cracks
in their feathers layered with shades
of earth and aviary gray delineated
hematite-black to match the vitreous
splendor of its eyes. Keratin beak, soft
as sunshine. It's song, simple.

When hot clouds came, the obscuration
wasn't much comfort. The chickadees
and wrens flew away. The warblers too.
The milky haze veiled even the bright
summer green, brown dirt in my garden
muted to dull beige.

Everything washed out when the rains
came in late fall. All is gray now. Where has
my little warbler gone? I only hear the chirps,
but I do remember the colors
                        of its song.

-John C. Mannone

John C. Mannone has work appearing/accepted in Azahares Literary Magazine, North Dakota Quarterly, Poetry South, Baltimore Review, Anacua Literary Arts Journal and others. He won the Jean Ritchie Fellowship (2017). He edits poetry for Abyss & Apex and other journals. A retired physics professor, he lives near Knoxville, TN. http://jcmannone.wordpress.com

# 9.

Es el dolor de un pueblo
el que **se desliza** en
la sangre de la tierra.

Acantilados bermejos
contienen **la angustia**
y las rítmicas palpitaciones.

**La gente murmura** en las
doradas esquinas de la ciudad,
se desliza la esperanza
con sutileza acuática.

¿dónde están los héroes del agua?
¿dónde las mujeres pez que **cantan en la aurora**?
¿dónde las ilusiones del nuevo amanecer?

*Todo se inunda.*

Escurre la lluvia
en los cristales,
de los acantilados
brota el agua densa.

*Canta, mujer pez, canta.*

-Xánath Caraza

# 9.

It is the people's pain
**sneaking** into
the blood of the land.

Crimson cliffs
contain the **anguish**
and rhythmic palpitations.

**People murmur** in the
golden corners of the city,
hope slips away
with aquatic subtlety.

where are the heroes of the water?
where the fish women and their **song of first light**?
where the illusions of the new dawn?

Everything becomes flooded.

**Rain** drips
down window panes,
dense water **sprouts**
from cliffs.

*Sing, fish woman, sing.*

-Xánath Caraza, translated by Sandra Kingery

Xánath Caraza is a traveler, educator, poet, short story writer, and translator. She writes for La Bloga, The Smithsonian Latino Center, Revista Literaria Monolito, and Seattle Escribe. In 2019 for the International Latino Book Awards she received Second Place for Hudson for "Best Book of Poetry in Spanish" and Second Place for Metztli for Best Short Story Collection. In 2018 for the International Latino Book Awards she received First Place for Lágrima roja for "Best Book of Poetry in Spanish by One Author" and First Place for Sin preámbulos / Without Preamble for "Best Book of Bilingual Poetry by One Author". Her book of poetry Syllables of Wind / Sílabas de viento received the 2015 International Book Award for Poetry. She was Writer-in-Residence at Westchester Community College, NY, 2016-2019. Caraza was the recipient of the 2014 Beca Nebrija para Creadores, Universidad de Alcalá de Henares in Spain. She was named number one of the 2013 Top Ten Latino Authors by LatinoStories.com. Her books of verse Where the Light is Violet, Black Ink, Ocelocíhuatl, Conjuro and her book of short fiction What the Tide Brings have won national and international recognition. Her other books of poetry are It Pierces the Skin, Balamkú, Fără preambul, Μαύρη μελάνη, Le sillabe del vento, Noche de colibríes, and Corazón pintado. Caraza has been translated into English, Italian, Romanian, and Greek; and partially translated into Nahuatl, Portuguese, Hindi, and Turkish.

# The revolving doors

Today I dream of you on the corners
on the boulevards of transparency
in the recesses of gray memories
where Tenochtitlan is confused with Uxmal
when I leave through the gate of Alcala in Madrid
but I cannot find you you've gotten lost as always
in Independence Square that connects with the Court
of the Lions in Granada where you've again gotten lost love

and I arrive to Buenos Aires
waiting for you in front of Teatro Colon
and you are in Guayaquil strolling along
the Guayas River awaiting me near the semicircle
of the Rotunda where Simon Bolívar and San Martin
shake hands but I am in the other esplanade the one
in Havana where I slip through the doors of the Cathedral
of the Immaculate Conception but you were waiting for me in

the First Cathedral of the Americas on Isabel La Católica Street
I exit the door and I almost catch you at the entrance to Machu Picchu
where you reappear in front of the San Juan Gate where you look dazed at the bay
and the fortresses I told you to wait for me at Angel Falls in Canaima Park
but you lost in Antigua in Tegucigalpa lost in the house of Neruda

to reveal this love that escapes me through the exits through the doors of forgetfulness
one stays open another stays closed and there we will remain with our hands extended
seeking to reinvent this sentiment on the revolving pages of history

*-Benito Pastoriza Iyodo*

Benito Pastoriza Iyodo is a poet residing in McAllen, TX. He writes about sexuality, social-political issues, and history. His published books are: Brothel of the word, A matter of men, September elegies, Waters of paradise, Letters to the shadow of your skin, Beloved, beloved of my heart. He has won numerous literary awards and his works are included in anthologies in various countries.

# Shipley Do-nuts

Mercy Rehab ventures a lick of glazed fingertip
holding back the bite 'til she can
recite one more reason why she deserves
the do-nut in front of her.

Chastity Brownbelt, recalling up to the coat closet
(real fur bare ass)
chases a post-blackout bearclaw with a cold blue razzberry tea

Mercy expects at noon to endure greedy hands,
probing her forgotten body, unmapped for so long until
her remaining son went up without the possibility of parole.

Chastity plucks baby spiders tangled in her neck hairs.
she cannot ascertain why the lady framed
by the plate glass engages her glazed
like a potentially deadly orgasm.

Mercy with her napkin on her lap,
registers epiphany with each delicate bite.
she loves this place
except when Sergio switches shifts with some stranger
who doesn't know how she likes it

-Anthony Hughes

Anthony Hughes was born with a pork chop around his neck. He married a wolf who made silver spoons for needy children. They built an empire from the wings of cruelty free butterflies.

# The Earth

To hold and nurture a seed;
To enroot it and soar in the sky,
Is the earth.

To ingrain a Man
With the virtue of Love
Is the earth.

To cut off the egos of a boasting man,
The outpour, tsunami, and quake
Is the earth.

The perfect balance of the Five Elements
To encompass humanity to eternity
Is the earth.

-Dr.Tejaswini Patil


Dr. Tejaswini Patil is an academician, poet and social worker; writes about Nature, social issues, feminist sensibilities and her experiences. Her books include, 'Talons and Nets', 'Verses of Silence', 'A Glass of Time' and 'Kaainat'. Part of the famous Coffee Table Book, 25 Women of Virtue. Awarded with 'Master of Creative Impulse' by World Poetry Conference, Punjab.

# LAUGH, DREAM

A dream of laughter sets me free,
wings and no clocks,
lighter than air and no keys anchoring;
for all my solitude,
I soar into the great unknown
and people greet me there;
the past is back in carefree uniform;
people drift through my mind
without the commensurate slinking;
the world flashes lightning
in the surrender of my eyes;
old places live in the highest color,
the fondest detail;
the immovable shifts ground,
the geraniums perk up,
the dead awake and thrash about in joy;
the moon is there for me to hitch a ride;
the sun is, once again, a willing servant;
beaches become trees become mountain trails
become pats on the back and then flowers and larks;
without constriction, the cradle bears the man,
the boy is father of the mother,
the child is on the job but just for the rewards,
not the heartbreak;
sure, it's all a lie
but how can it not be;

savory smells return to the kitchens;
backyards teem with boys;
a girl smiles at me from the edge of oblivion,
pulls me to safety as I fall;
I'm here where the day glows,
where the night sings;
events breathe.
friends fill familiar spaces,
family gather, enormous and round;
a dream of laughter.
who cares if morning's lurking;
I will wake with all my life for company;
a dream of laughter
eschews compromise.

*-John Grey*

John Grey is an Australian poet, US resident. Recently published in That, Dalhousie Review and North Dakota Quarterly with work upcoming in Qwerty, Chronogram and failbetter.

# Mountain time

Where the mountain joins the valley shadows run flooding
Time is suspended, the present written in lines rhyming and strange
Paths into obscurity hide the traces of lost things
Passing into this false night I find sweet sad dreams
That rise and fade like waves lighted by sun streams
When I join words into rhyme it is in this land
In dark valleys and caves such as most forget
As I walk this path my steps go beyond love and reason
There at the base of the world among the bones of the land
I rest with the stones and look up to see light above

-Laura Moverin

Laura is a queer Brisbane based writer and artist. She works as a librarian and so a love of words and literature is a hazard of her profession. Laura also helps run a writers group for teenagers. She majored in History and Literature but writes purely for her own pleasure.

# A query

There is a dither incarnated into hesitancy
A no- name- feeling, expressed into lingo
Something biting sharply with the teeth of the query
I don't stay even though the evil pushes me to go

My answers a little baby not older than primary kids
The voice meandering towards the mouse hole
My echo over yours freely skids
We, both need the believe, tomorrow will be a whole

We have to hope and believe, we
Even though a dither is incarnated into hesitancy!

-*Erenestina Halili*



Ms. Erenestina Gjergji Halili, is a professor at the Faculty of History and Philology, in the department of Language and Literature, Tirana, Albania. Ms.Halili received the "Doctor of Philological Sciences" degree in 2012. Ms. Erenestina Gjergji Halili, is the author of four books: "Gjama e erës", "Bibliography of the published Albanian Drama (the first study in the field of Albanian dramaturgy, in Albania, Kosovo, Macedonia, Montenegro, etc.), poetic book "Bibulz", and monographic study "Scanderbeg-dramaticus heros, Theatrum Mundi".

# ay, Padre Viento

     speak to us.
teach us, once again.

Through the rustle
     Of your trees
you whisper wisdom
     and it roams the earth
          in all its languages,
   in all its accents.
you sign your name in the waters,
in the ripples of the lakes and rivers
     you put an exclamation point to your words.

yet we have turned our ears away,
     we have abandoned your language.
we are lost.

in our impudence and our arrogance,
we have disowned our earth family.
our rivers and oceans cry out to us.
     our forest and sky are no longer
that which you gave us.

Forgive us.

-Pablo Pineda

Pablo Pineda is a recent writer of poetry. He writes of his family's experiences as migrant workers throughout Texas. He was born in Mc Allen, Texas, a first generation U.S. citizen.

# Children have left the house

the timid streams gather courage
bustle as they build momentum.
they start to join at the junctions
and begin to smoothen all the rocks
one at a time. sandstone is becoming
quartzite. granite is becoming gneiss.
milk is curdling and the
tributaries are forming a river.
A river which is uninhibited.
It has no color, no nationality,
no race, no religion. it breaks
all the boxes ,crashes mental dams,
while it houses the salmons and eels,
It is the home for fishes and flies,
a place for hippos and rhinos
but has no place for a thought
of flowing backwards.

-Jay Gandhi


Jay Gandhi has been writing poetry since the age of 6. His journey started when he became an active member of the poetry forum poetrycircle.com. Inputs from seasoned poets helped him edit his drafts and slowly he developed his own poetic voice. His Indian background is the spice in his poetry.

# TWO

**The Truth-Tellers**

# Half and Half

We're in a Mexican restaurant in the grout between central and downtown Brownsville.
We sit divided by three strips of Saltillo tile from the family next to us,
the family that looks like they belong here,
with two big silver balloons, nueve y cero.
They are celebrating almost a century of life.

We sit at a table where a family member asks, "do they have burgers here, or something?"
I sit between my parents like a border town.

I want to say gracias when the waiter brings a bowl of limes
but the *r* unfurls on my tongue before I can even say it,
and I become a gringa with no accent–
at least, not one to be proud of.

I ask for a refill and resist the urge to ask my mom to speak for me.
I don't want to hear myself speak here.
I'm ashamed of my "por favor" because half an accent
is only half a culture, and half is not enough.

My uncle–I don't say "tio"–tells us he thinks we're being ignored by the waiter
"because we're gringos."

I am offended he would assume *my* people would avoid another's existence,
would deny him service because of his skin, like he may do to us.

The man turning ninety sits at the head of his table
in a yellow suit coat with pills of wear and tear on his back like beads of sweat.
It's something I've probably seen when I've shopped downtown
at the thrift store whose sections are labeled in Spanish first, in large red letters,
and English second, in small black letters in parentheses.
In Brownsville, I live inside parentheses.

Someone at our table says "mucho bueno" to our waiter,
and he walks away. She laughs at herself, at her idea of a joke.
It's funny to speak their language…my language? No.
Only half of it is mine, and to me, half is not enough.

*-Sofia Zamora-Wiley*




Sofia Zamora-Wiley is a 17-year-old poet from Brownsville, Texas. She enjoys writing poetry, fiction, essays, and even music, and she's always eager to share her love and passion for all forms of creative expression with others, and she's extremely honored to be a featured youth poet at VIPF this year.

# Undying Love

You hold the key to my heart forever,
With a ferocious glance full of promise.
To love and cherish me whatsoever
No matter the obstacles upon us.
A vow made from one heart to another
Securing timelessness, love of two hearts.
Bestowing brilliant eyes for only each other,
Creating love purer than the fine arts.
I reside near your presence, I adore

Living side by side in eternal bliss.
Until death do us part forever more,
At long last we may share our very first kiss.
As long as I shall live you are my love;
Even when my time comes to rise above.

-Emily Lara

Emily Lara is a fifteen year old poet. Reading and writing are some of her biggest passions. Her parents are her biggest inspirations and supporters when it comes to writing. She loves creating a world where other people can relate to and be inspired from.

# Fractured and Twisted

Staying up late at night, waiting
for your warm and gentle embrace.
Tossing and turning and only finding,
an emptiness full of pure and utter heartbreak.
I miss your kind and gentle smirk
That used to leave me unequivocally speechless.
Once upon a time, I trusted your judgement
And your word without a single
Ounce of hesitation.
Now all that is left is pure outrage
At someone who never cared,
About the broken pieces left behind.
Left alone with pain and suffering,
Endless flowing of tears at your name.
Begging to be let free from the cage,
You tried to put them behind.
Whispering out in pain,
For all of my suffering to dissipate.
I beg you to set me free,
All I am is an empty shell
Of a broken, messed up
Twisted version of myself.

-Emily Lara

Emily Lara is a fifteen year old poet. Reading and writing are some of her biggest passions. Her parents are her biggest inspirations and supporters when it comes to writing. She loves creating a world where other people can relate to and be inspired from.

# Happiness

Happy came to visit me
He brought friends along the way
I told them to leave
But he told me it'll all be ok
So i told him i loved him more than life itself
And he told me he wanted me too
They laid me down on the sharp springs and there i stayed
For days and years
I waited
My flesh rotting like an old flower
Putrid and pale
The animals came and kissed me
And took bits and pieces
I felt loved
I felt needed
I felt him inside of me

-Dorian Ramirez

Dorian Ramirez was born on October 9th 2004 and is a freshman at La Joya Early College High School and likes to write about how he's feeling and situations that he finds interesting. He hopes to continue writing and is excited for the future.

# Abuelo

El día que te enfermaste
 Se me rompió el corazón
Estuviste enfermo por un tiempo,
Entonces Dios decidió ganar otro ángel en el cielo

Sólo me queda tu recuerdo
Tus manos trabajadoras y tus ojos brillosos
Eras mi todo, iluminaste mi día
La persona a la que me gustaría ver
 todos los días después de la escuela

Tomaste un pedazo de mi corazón contigo,
Y nadie reemplazará ese pedazo perdido
Gracias por estar ahí para mí cuando más te necesitaba

-*Jaivette Sepulveda*

Jaivette Sepulveda was born on November 16th 2003 and is 16 years old. She is the daughter of Jaime and Elizabeth Sepulveda. She is currently a 10th grader at La Joya Early College High School. Jaivette Sepulveda is from Palmview, Texas.

# Adolescencia

Esta bien
Esta bien no ser perfecta
Está bien ser tu misma
Esta bien no ser tan linda como las otras chicas
Eso es lo que me digo

Esta bien no ser tan lista como las demas
Está bien tener problemas
Esta bien ser insegura
Eres perfecta como eres
Eso es lo que me digo

Trata de no estresarte tanto
Se que la vida es difícil en este momento
Pero mejorara
Siempre lo hace
Todo estara bien

-*Kristal Vivas*

Kristal Vivas tiene 14 años. Sus padres se llaman Jose and Laura Vivas. Ella atiende La Joya Early College High School.

# Rainy days

Splat, splat, splat,
The sound of the rain hitting the metal roof
As I lay on my bed
Reminiscing about the times I spent with you
The smell of dirt as the rain hits the ground is fragrant
My memories with you are still fuzzy,
but whenever it rains,
I am yet reminded of you
Splat, splat, splat
The sound of the rain as it hits the sidewalk
Splat, splat, splat
The sound of my shoes as I run towards you
Splat, splat, splat
The ever ending sound I hear when I think of you
I close my window shut and play my music
Hoping it will drown out the sound of the rain
So i can finally stop thinking about you

-*Victoria Salinas*

Victoria Salinas is from Sullivan City, TX. She attends La Joya Early College High School. Her hobbies are spending time with friends and family. She was born on September 10, 2004 in Mission, TX

# Abuela

Tu eres la mejor abuela que existe
Pelo corto y color castaño
Ojos entre gris y cafe

tu piel es arrugada como las sabanas de la cama
tus manos rasposas, probablemente por hacernos
 tantas tortillas de harina

Cuando estoy afuera de tu casa
puedo escuchar los pericos
que has tenido desde que yo era pequeña

El aire que sopla se siente diferente
Se siente más ligero, se siente más limpio
El aire que sopla huele a los rosales color rosa
que tienes en la entrada de tu casa

Al entrar a tu casa puedo oler las
tortillas de harina recién hechas a mano
Que nos has hecho a todos
Abuela eres la mejor
Y todos lo saben.

-*Yathcire Arredondo*

Yathcire Arredondo nació el 17 de septiembre de 2004 y ahora tiene 15 años. Yathcire se encuentra actualmente en noveno grado en La Joya Early College High School y es residente de MIssion, Texas.

# Una estrella para mí

Eres una brillante persona y
muy importante persona en mi vida.
Eres una persona muy grande en mí corazón.
Siempre me has estado viendo me
 crecer en mis logros y en mis caídas.
Cuando no me podía sostener a mi misma
 tú estabas allí para levantarme.

Tu me alumbras mis días y
 noches con solo una sonrisa.
Tu me guias como una brújula para tomar
 un buen camino y también para hacer buenas decisiones.

Eres tan grande como una estrella en el universo.
Gracias por siempre estar en mi vida mamá.


-*Alexandra Cerda*




Alexandra Cerda is 17 years old and is currently a senior at La Joya Early College High School. She was born on July 9, 2002. Her poem is dedicated to her mom.

# Stars

When the sun rests it's blinding glare
the dark sky starts to cry
billions and billions of shining tears
lighting up the path before me
watching as the creatures of the night take me away to extinction
watching as I reach out for help

oh how beautiful the stars are
bright souls up in the sky
will I become a star once the creature stops hurting me ?
or would I be left here on the cold , muddy ground , wishing for it to be over ?
all I can do for now is stare up at the stars as my vision gets blurry

when the creature finally looms over me one last time before taking it's step back to the silent night
I couldn't help but reach up
up at the twinkling lights
 up at the souls watching
up at the stars
oh how beautiful the stars were

-Kathlyn Duberney

Kathlyn Duberney was born on December 2, 2004. She is the youngest of three siblings and she is currently a 9th grader in La Joya Early College.

# Letter to My Parents

I know I may seem happy
I know that I get home with a smile on my face
I don't get to see Mom much anymore since she started working
I don't really have anyone to talk to at home anymore
With dad's condition, he can't' feel many emotions

Anyway, I'm writing this to let you know
I'm going through so much right now
And I don't know how to cope with it
It's hard
Really, really hard
Who knew growing up would be such a sad process
Some people are good with dealing with the pain
And just my luck, I'm the type of person who would like to be alone and cry

Mom
Dad
All I ask is that the next time you see me sad
Just hug me
Remind me I'm not alone
I know I'm really hard-headed sometime
I don't mean to
I'm a teen – it's normal
I'm sorry if I behave badly at times
I'm growing and learning

Just know I love and care about you both

*-Koral Lezama*

Koral Lezama is a student from Progreso High School.

# Media Naranja

Es la manera
que tu sonrisa
me busca,
aunque observando el mundo este

Anhelo esos momentos
cuando las estrellas de tu rostro
sobre mi ser brillan;
mi vida alumbran.

Alma buena eres.
Si te dare mis tesoros,
los regresarás multiplicados.
Cuidarás lo que me mantiene viva.

Guardaras cada secreto
tatuado en nuestra piel
por la tinta de cada susurro
en momentos privados compartidos

Como Don Quijote a Rocinante
Te amare. Ciega, sin duda.
Pero será un amor resplandeciente;
un amor eterno será el nuestro

Cada cosa que anhelo de ti,
juro que lo haré igualmente

Todo esto
Podría convertirse en verdad
Solo tendrías que
Anhelarlo también

-*Darissa Rodriguez*

Darissa Rodriguez is a senior in high school (a youth submission). She has been writing poetry for over five years, and this is her first year sharing her poetry with others. Her poems express the topics of love, culture and upbringing.

# Border Town Tongue

Oh how I wish I could
slide the sounds off my tongue,
naturally,
as if it were her home.
Like honey from a promised land
Never reached:
I long for that sweetness
to pour out from my lips

But ah
Prejudice,
constructed a
Border Wall in my brain
a tollway on my tongue.

-*Darissa Rodriguez*

Darissa Rodriguez is a senior in high school (a youth submission). She has been writing poetry for over five years, and this is her first year sharing her poetry with others. Her poems express the topics of love, culture and upbringing.

## Dear Anonymous

I wanted to tell you how great of a person you are
You're so loving
The way your smile is like a night light is amazing
When you talk it's a symphony
Your eyes are country stars lighting up the dark
Every time you hug me
It warms me up from the inside
It's unbelievable the way you make me feel
I turn like a tomato every time we talk
When you grab my hand it's like if my hand got soaked in a pillow full of feathers
So soft and warm
Just perfect
You're such a beautiful person inside and out
Just wanted to write about what I think of and about you

-Joanna Hinojosa

Joanna Hinojosa is from Santa Maria and is fourteen years old. She likes to play basketball and softball for the Progreso Red Ants.

# Anónimo

Nunca pensé que te encontraría
Nunca pensé en volverte a ver
Pero así fue

No digo que sea malo
En realidad me siento feliz
A lo mejor no me creerás

Pero,
En ti encontré lo que nunca imaginé
Lo que no sabía que quería
Y ahí es cuando entendí
Después de una decepción, siempre llega una nueva ilusión

*-Ashley Olvera*

Ashley Olvera tiene 15 años y estudia en la joya early college. Su cumpleaños es en agosto 16 de 2004, le gusta pasar tiempo con familia y amigos. Sueña con graduarse e ir a colegio.

# My sunflower

You've been with me through everything,
Through the good and the bad
And you have helped me overcome things,
I never thought I could, you have nurtured me,
You have taken me to where I am today,
To the person I am today.
You are like a sunflower,
You have always been a brilliant person,
And someone who has always encouraged others to make an effort
Additional and motivate them to improve and make her children
To succeed in life,
I am always grateful that you never gave up on us
I will always love and appreciate you.

-Aylin Gonzalez

Aylin Gonzalez was born on September 27th, 2004 and is 15 years old. She is the daughter of Roel Gonzalez and Beatriz Gonzalez. Currently, she is a 10th grader at La Joya Early College High School and a resident of Mission, Texas.

# Wasn't her

I was walking holding hands with her, dropping her off to her class.
We locked eyes and she told me she loved me.
A month ago I would've said I loved her back,
But I had to stop lying to her and myself.
I had to understand that I wasn't capable of loving her anymore.
She asked me why,
There really wasn't reason,
I just didn't want her anymore.
I didn't want to hurt her feelings.
I felt like she just wasn't for me.
I let go of her hand and told her it just wasn't gonna work.
I didn't really know what I meant by that.
I didn't stop loving her yesterday,
Nor a week ago,
Nor a month ago,
Honestly I don't think I even loved her at all.

-Adolfo Acosta

Adolfo Acosta is in tenth grade, and he is 15 years old and goes to La Joya Early College High School.

# Dear Dad,

I wanted to tell you that I miss you so much. Every day that passes by I always ask myself *why did you have to die so soon?* My life without you is so hard. I need you here with me. I need your advice. Every day that I go to school I feel sad because we used to text each other every class period. I really miss spending time with you like when we used to when you were still alive. Like when we used to go hunting together and also when we would go fishing every Sunday morning. I loved going hunting with you because we used to shoot the bunnies or the birds with our guns. All of this comes to mind every time I'm remembering you and it really affects me not having you by my side anymore. Dad, I love you so much. I need you with me even though you're not here with me. I want you to take care of me from the sky wherever I go all my life. I will go stay there with you forever and we could do the things that we used to do. I miss you so much, Dad, and I love you so much. Hopefully, I will see you someday.
See you later, Dad. Bye.

-Brian Ramirez



Brian Ramirez is a student at Progreso High School. He enjoys playing soccer and video games. He hopes to one day do the things he used to do with his dad

# Te vi de nuevo

Vi esos ojos tiernos y esas manos suaves
Las manos con las que me acariciabas
Esas caricias falsas que no tenía sentido
Traté de no llorar, de no volver a caer
Empecé a recordar de todas las veces que me hacías sentir que no valía la pena
Todas esas veces que lloraba en mi cuarto porque no sabía cómo hacerte feliz
Te daba todo de mí todos los días cuando tú no dabas nada
Todos decían que no valías la pena
Al final no me importó porque lo único que me importaba eras tú
Cuando te decía lo que sentía, tú solo te callabas en vez de ayudarme
Yo era la única que decía que te amaba mientras tú no decías nada
Me dejaste después de todo lo que yo hice por ti y tenía coraje
Coraje porque tú me dejaste cuando yo hice todo por nosotros cuando tú no hiciste nada- Me sentía quebrantada sin fuerzas, así lo pasé durante meses

Vino un día en donde alguien vino a mi vida tenía miedo
Al final él fue el que me sacó de esta tristeza
Me siento amada y importante por primera vez
Él está conmigo cuando dudo de mí misma
Él me dice que me ama todos los dias y me hace sonreír

Y no llorar como tú lo hacías
Sus caricias son tan tiernas y con mucho sentimiento
A veces pienso que por qué no fuiste tú el que me trató así
Pero al fin lo comprendí,
Tú sólo estabas conmigo para no sentirte solo no porque sentías lo mismo que yo
Te vi,
Vi esos ojos tiernos y esas manos suaves
Pero ahora no me importa porque al final,
Encontré lo que buscaba

-*Britani De La Rosa*

Britani De La Rosa was born on March 31, 2004 in Monterrey, Nuevo Leon, Mexico. She is currently a 10th grader in La Joya Early College High School.

# I saw you again

I saw those tender eyes and those soft hands
The hands with which you caressed me
Those fake caresses that made no sense
I tried not to cry, not to fall again
I started remembering all the times you made me feel it wasn't worth it
All those times I cried in my room because I didn't know how to make you happy
I gave you all of me every day when you didn't give anything
Everyone said you were not worth it
In the end I didn't care because the only thing that mattered was you
When I told you what I felt, you just shut up instead of helping me
I was the only one who said I loved you while you said nothing
You left me after everything I did for you and I had courage
Courage because you left me when I did everything for us when you didn't do anything- I felt broken without strength, I went through it for months

A day came when someone came into my life I was afraid
In the end he was the one who got me out of this sadness
I feel loved and important for the first time
He is with me when I doubt myself
He tells me that he loves me every day and makes me smile
And don't cry like you did

His caresses are so tender and with a lot of feeling
Sometimes I think why it was not you who treated me like this
But I finally understood
You were just with me to not feel alone not because you felt the same as me
I saw you,
I saw those tender eyes and those soft hands
But now I don't care because in the end,
I found what I was looking

-Britani De La Rosa

Britani De La Rosa was born on March 31, 2004 in Monterrey, Nuevo Leon, Mexico. She is currently a 10th grader in La Joya Early College High School.

# Tiempo

Sé que tienes miedo
Sé que has sido lastimado
Sé que no has dejado ir el pasado
Pero te esperaré
Te esperaré, no importa cuánto tiempo pase
Esperaré por tu amor
Ahora el tiempo ha pasado
Finalmente dejaste ir al pasado
Finalmente podemos ser felices juntos
   Finalmente puedo hacerte sentir amado como ninguna otra mujer te ha hecho sentir
Finalmente puedo hacerte feliz
Finalmente eres mio
Para siempre
Solamente te pido un favor
Por favor no me rompas el corazón como los hombre del pasado
Que yo también he sido lastimada

-*Evelyn D. Cuevas*

Evelyn D. Cuevas and she is from Sullivan City, Texas. Her parents are Cynthia and Manuel Cuevas. She is currently a junior at La Joya Early College High School.

# La vida del portero

Un portero nace siendo portero
Hay que tener un don especial y una valentía fuera de lo normal
Para ponerse por voluntad propia debajo de una portería
Por eso es difícil encontrar un portero al que le guste su trabajo
Y por lo mismo, la vida del portero no es nada sencilla

Un portero sacrifica su vida en cada partido
Con golpes contra el suelo, el jugador y hasta el poste
Estos golpes aparatosos suelen llevarse al portero
Y a causa de esos golpes, la personalidad del portero es tan diferente a la del resto
Y por lo mismo, la vida del portero no es nada sencilla

Siempre el portero es un jugador aparte
Que vive en una hábitat natural propia, el área
Su vida siempre está al margen del error
Y el entrenamiento no los ayuda con su aspecto psicológico
Y por lo mismo, la vida del portero no es nada sencilla

El error o fallo de un delantero, media o defensa no es nada
Pero una mala salida o bloqueada forma una gran alteración en el campo
El error o fallo de un portero suelen costar goles
Y detrás de ese error o fallo vienen las criticas a toda velocidad
Y por lo mismo, la vida del portero no es nada sencilla

-Yasaira G. Herrera

Yasaira G. Herrera was born on January 23, 2002, and is 18 years old. She is the daughter of Juan and María Herrera. She is currently a senior at La Joya Early College High School, and is the starter goalkeeper for the Lady Coyotes Varsity Soccer Team.

# Crash

I couldn't look at him
Someone that bled and cried
How can I look at someone
That has scars around his hands
I saw him cry and yell in agony
He got hurt
And I couldn't help him

I wish I could
I wish I was there to tell him
"Everything will be fine"
But yet he'll still cry, and say
"Make it stop…"

I'm sorry I couldn't help you
I wish I could, but I couldn't
Please forget me
                I can't stand this
                          Please make this stop..

I wish your scars around
        Your head and hands
Can disappear just like I did


-Mel Cedillo

Mel Cedillo is a student from Progreso High School. She writes drama based on popular anime and likes long walks on the beach.

# The Bus Stop

On a cold rainy night
Underneath the lamp post
Close to the bus stop
There was an old man
Sitting on a sidewalk

I got out of my car
Decided to go and help
But when I got there
Something surprise me
I couldn't believe what I saw

The old man was wearing all white
With his hair really long and black
He had his hair over his face
I tried to see his face and moved
His hair to the back

Next thing I know I'm floating
And I see my body on the ground
The old man tells me…
Welcome to Ghost Town

-Mario Sosa

Mario Sosa is fifteen years old. He likes sports and wings.

# ALONE

We all don't know life is a joke. We all suffer deep down in our deep AF bodies. Many people just see our outside, they think we are happy. But on the inside we are all DYING FROM PAIN. Everyone thinks that life is to just spend time with the most important people.... Family.... Others say it is to have the most enjoyable time of your life. We all know it is going to end someday. We all have friends, family, and loved ones. We all know that death will soon come to us. Everyone we know will not be here. It'll only be us who are alone in the dark, suffering from our closest people's death. We all suffer in the dark and many never make it out of the darkness. They get so used to the darkness that it is their new home. A home to where no one can bother them. Some don't make it out alive at all. Not all people you see happy are actually happy. They seem happy to not get bothered by anyone. People have problems with many things – crowded places, having to talk to other people, etc. Some make it out, but others manage to stay.

WE ALL ARE ALONE!

-*Jose Ramos*

Jose Ramos likes Color Guard and likes to play games. He also enjoys listening to music.

# Mi gran amigo

Mi querido perrito,
su nombre era Oso,
mi gran compañero,
cómplice y amoroso.

Creciste a mi lado,
te recuerdo con gran cariño,
me cuidabas fuertemente,
de lo que creías un peligro.

Un día me abandonaste,
tu camino termino,
mi corazón destrozaste,
aunque mi vida siguió.

Ya han pasado 5 años,
y te recuerdo como si fuera ayer,
el gran tiempo que pasamos,
nunca te olvidare…

-*Celsa Treviño*

Celsa Treviño tiene dieciséis años y es estudiante de undécimo grado. Le gusta participar en los servicios comunitarios de la escuela. Actualmente está en las organizaciones de Society of Hispanic Professional Engineers y Mu Alpha Theta National High School Mathematics Honor Society.

# Ya no siento nada por tí

Un dia dijiste que me querias
Un dia dijiste que nunca me harías daño
Un dia dijiste que tenias miedo a perderme
Un dia dijiste que jamas me engañarias

Y es triste ver que todo esto eran solo mentiras
Ver que la única persona que pensé que no me haría daño
Me dejo echa en mil pedazos

Llegue a entregarte mi corazón
Y al parecer a ti no te importo
Llegue a enfrentar a mis padres solo por tí
Y al final ni la pena valio

Tus mensajes cada día eran más secos
Tu interes hacia mi iba descendiendo

Y pensar que trate de todo
Para que lo de nosotros durará años
Pero ni a los 3 meses llegamos

Me costo mucho superarte
Pero estoy feliz
Porque despues de tanto tiempo
Puedo decir que ya no siento nada por tí

-*Evelin Olivares*

Evelin Olivares nació el 31 de julio de 2003 y tiene 16 años. Es hija de Margarita Gracia y Lucio Olivares. Actualmente es estudiante de 11° grado en La Joya Early College High School.

# Nature

Nature is beautiful every time I look outside
And I look at that beautiful landscape that many people enjoy
Walking the beautiful view at sunset that falls in love with the
Eyes of any person and at night feeling the beautiful breeze
Air coming from those gigantic trees that line that beautiful
forest, the creatures that abound among the trees, deer and
bears abound.
That place you can see animals jumping through the trees
some tender squirrels that abound the place, people camping
enjoying their vacations
Tourists touring the river observing the beautiful fish swimming
like
Beautiful mermaids, at dusk look at the beautiful clear sky and
observe
The beautiful stars and planets that adorn the sky and the forest
are a beautiful place that many people enjoy walking.

-Hector Flores

Hector Flores is an average teen in La Joya Early College High School and he really enjoys playing games and spending time with his family and friends.

# Sí, Hispano

-No, no soy Mexicano.
Sí, yo nací aquí.
Mexi-ameri-cuh, Hispano.

No, no soy ilegal.
No, no salté el muro.
No, no crucé nadando.
No, no soy una mala persona.

Sí, mis padres son Mexicanos.
-Eso explica tu piel morena.
¿Por qué no eres bajo en altura?
-No, no necesito bigote.
Sí, ojos marrones.

Sí, son horribles los rumores que hacen de nosotros.
No, no violo a la gente.
No, no corto pasto para vivir,
Ni siquiera soy suficientemente mayor para trabajar.

No, no sé dónde comprar panchos.
No, no se dónde comprar sombreros de mariachi.
Pero sí sé dónde comprar tacos.
No, no los de Taco Bell,
Tacos de verdad.

Sí, soy religioso.
Sí, mi mamá ora.
No, no es bruja,
Esa gran olla es sólo pozole.
No, no como frijoles con todas mis comidas.
Sí, una tortilla también es cuchara.

Sí, somos diferentes.
Sí, somos similares.

Sí, Hispano.

-*Emmanuel Ayala*

Emmanuel Ayala nació el 25 de mayo de 2004. Es hijo de Luis y Alejandra Ayala. Actualmente es estudiante de décimo grado en La Joya Early College High School y es parte de NHS, Mu Alpha Theta, SHPE y la banda.

# Yes, Hispanic

No, I am not Mexican.
Yes, I was born here.
Mexi-ameri-cuh, Hispanic.

No, I'm not illegal.
No, I didn't jump the wall.
No, I didn't come here swimming.
No, I'm not a bad person.

Yes, my parents are mexican.
"That explains your brown skin."
"How come you're not short."
No, I don't need a mustache.
Yes, brown eyes.

Yeah, it's awful the rumors you make of us.
No, I don't rape people.
No, I don't cut grass for a living.
I'm not even old enough to work.

No, I don't know where to buy panchos.
No, I don't know where to buy big mariachi hats.
But I do know where to buy tacos.
No, not from Taco Bell,
Real tacos.

Yes, I am religious.
Yes, my mom prays.
No, she's not a witch.
That big pot is just pozole..

No, don't eat beans with everything.
Yes, a tortilla is also a spoon.

Yes, I am different.
Yes, we are similar.

Yes, Hispanic.

-*Emmanuel Ayala*

Emmanuel Ayala was born on May 25, 2004. He is the son of Luis and Alejandra Ayala. He is currently a 10th grader at La Joya Early College High School and is part of NHS, Mu Alpha Theta, SHPE, and band.

# I wait

I wait.
I wait as the wind howls
Like a wolf at night.
I wait till the birds chirp the same
The way they did when you were with me.
I wait till my worlds feels
Complete again.
I wait till it gets better without your
Company even though I know that day won't come.
I wait till the day you might
Come back to me.
I wait forever and always.
I wait.

-Damian Ramirez

Damian is a freshman at La Joya Early College. Damian was born on march 13, 2005 and is 15 years old. Damian's poem is about how life is without someone you care about.

# El Rancho

Antes contaba historias mi abuelita
De cómo vino siendo el rancho.
Contaba de historias bonitas.
Me decía cuentos de gente con palabra.
Y de cómo antes de dinero,
Lo que un huevo les compraba.
Contaba del esfuerzo de mi bisabuelo.
Pero cuando se acabaron ellos.
Y con los años,
El rancho se separa,
Cercas por donde quiera,
Lo que queda es un triste callejón.
La palabra se la lleva el viento,
Hambre de tierra,
Corre por sus mentes.
Crece la envidia
Señores sin respeto a la herencia.
Familia separada,
Primos ya viejos.
En cualquier momento se acerca la muerte,
Ninguna señal de perdón ni amor.
El karma existe
Al final sólo tres metros tendremos.

-*Emily Peña*

Emily Peña was born November 11, 2001 in Mission Texas. Her parents are Rosalinda Pruneda and Gerardo Peña. She is currently a senior in La Joya Early College High School.

# The Ranch

My grandmother used to tell me stories
Of how the ranch came to be.
She told beautiful stories.
She told me stories of people with words.
And how before money,
What an egg would buy for them.
She would tell me of my great grandfather's efforts.
But when they ran out.
And over the years,
The ranch separates,
Fences everywhere
All that remains is a sad alleyway.
The word is blown away by the wind,
Hunger of land,
Run through their minds.
Envy grows
Elder men without respect to the inheritance.
Family separating,
Cousins of old age.
At any moment death approaches,
And no sign of forgiveness or love.
Karma exists
In the end only six feet deep we will have.

-Emily Peña

Emily Peña was born November 11, 2001 in Mission Texas. Her parents are Rosalinda Pruneda and Gerardo Peña. She is currently a senior in La Joya Early College High School.

# Para siempre

Pensé que duraríamos para siempre
Hasta llenarnos de arrugas
Siempre nos reíamos de lo mismo
Nos gustaba lo mismo
Y siempre planeamos futuras metas

Hasta que los rumores comenzaron
Primero en silencio y después en grupos se pasaron
Empezamos a dudar y más a desconfiar de sí
Poco a poco nos fuimos separando
Y como las manecillas del reloj nos desviamos más

De tiempo a tiempo nos topamos
Al mirarnos, nos sonreímos; como si fuera una escena retrospectiva
Recordatorios de buenos momentos, risas y momentos nos golpearon
Como si nada hubiera pasado, seguimos caminando sin preguntar

Pense que durariamos para siempre
Mejores amigas por siempre...

-Angie Rodas

Angie Rodas is currently a student at La Joya Early College, beginning to write her own poems has turned into a passion and sees them as a way to express herself, her surroundings and what is happening in the world.

# Potholes

Life has vast potholes
Only you know whether to jump or not
Would you give up if a bump is too big?
Or you would jump it like it was a pool

There are many potholes at school,
Like friends
Sometimes we fight and sometimes we love each other
Sometimes we argue about insignificant things
But we still have fun

Life has potholes, just like families
Why is there vowing marriages, if there's divorces
Why love someone, then betray them by going behind their backs with someone else
Why is the world manipulative, cruel, and unforgiving we say
Why fall in temptation if they won't be responsible for a baby

There are many potholes in the world
Should we continue studying or not?
Should I do what makes me happy or what makes my parents proud?
Will I follow my own path or others?
When will everyone be satisfied?
What is one's life purpose?
Do I really feel like waking up?

Life has vast potholes
And these are just a few.

*-Angie Rodas*

Angie Rodas is currently a student at La Joya Early College, beginning to write her own poems has turned into a passion and sees them as a way to express herself, her surroundings and what is happening in the world.

# Los mas feos

Somos los mas feos
Y rechazó la opinión de que
Somos tan hermosas como las modelos que muestran
Entiendo que esto puede ser una sorpresa, pero
Todos somos preciosos
Es una mentira
La fealdad y la arrogancia lucharán
En 16 años, les diré a mis hijos que
Mi principal prioridad es la fealdad porque
Ser feo
Es más importante que
Ser considerado
Te digo esto:
Érase una vez
Todos se preocuparán unos por otros
Pero esto no será cierto en mi generación.
Todos son egoístas tan pronto como nacen
Especialistas me dijeron
Ser agnóstico ayudará
Yo no creo que
Las personas compasivas sobrevivirán
En el futuro,
La depresión mundial gobernará
Ya no se puede decir que
Las personas corteses estarán vivas
Será obvio que

Los arrogantes y la hermosura se hará cargo
Es una tontería suponer que
Las personas modestas sobrevivirán
(Abajo hacia arriba)

*-Angie Rodas*

Angie Rodas is currently a student at La Joya Early College, beginning to write her own poems has turned into a passion and sees them as a way to express herself, her surroundings and what is happening in the world.

# You

I remember the first time I saw you.
Your soft black hair with your nice brown eyes and big smile.
We became friends before I even got to second period.
You were there for me when no one else was.
We were friends for a long time before it all changed.
Little did we know it would change us forever
Or more importantly how it would change me forever.
I don't love anymore.
I don't trust anymore.
I don't commit anymore.
It hurts knowing you moved on and left me behind
Like the wind flowing in between the trees.
All the memories we had, all the laughs we shared
Washed away like the ocean waves.
All the times I talked about you to my friends and family
Gone just like the sun at sunset.
I remember the first time I saw you.

-Miranda Flores

Miranda Flores was born on September 27, 2004. Her parents are Olga Flores and Erwin Flores. She is a 9th grader who attends La Joya Early College High School in La Joya, Texas.

# Mi Abuela

Mi abuela
quien se sienta en su jardín verde
escucha a los pájaros cantar
mira las hojas caer
ellas aterrizan con facilidad
delicadas gotas de agua sobre los lirios
Mi abuela
cuyas plantas son suaves
tal como ella
mirando el sol ponerse
el jardin con ella
Mi abuela
quien se sienta en su jardín
escucha el golpeteo de la lluvia
en el suelo
Mi abuela
quien se sienta en su jardín.

-*Liliana Mendez*

Liliana Mendez is a 14-year-old-girl, who is currently a 9th grader at La Joya Early College High School. Liliana loves to read, write books, poems, and short stories.

# My Grandma

My grandma
who sits in her garden
listens to the birds sing
watches the leaves fall down
they land with ease
delicate water drops on the lillies
my grandma
whose plants are gentle
just like her
watching the sun go down
the garden with her
My grandma
who sits in her garden
listens to the rain patter
on the soil
My grandma
who sits in her garden.

-Liliana Mendez

Liliana Mendez is a 14-year-old-girl, who is currently a 9th grader at La Joya Early College High School. Liliana loves to read, write books, poems, and short stories.

# Amor Verdadero

Hay un punto en la vida de un hombre
Donde se da cuenta de un amor verdadero
Cuando ve por primera vez a su hija
sus primeros pasos,analizando cada uno
Con cuidado y estando allí por si se cae
Agarrado de la mano,la lleva a su clase de
 primer grado...más nervioso que ella.
Cada año el amor del padre aumenta
Ella ya no es una niña,sino una jóven
Sentado orgullosamente,viendo como
Su hija sonríe con su diploma en el aire.
Ahora sigue la vida verdadera,donde
Se acordará de los consejos de su padre
Agarrado del brazo de la novia,entregandola
Al hombre que compartirá su amor con
Ya no es niña,ni tampoco joven...ella es
Una mujer,una mujer que enseñó un hombre el
Amor verdadero...el amor del padre…

-Abigail Díaz


Abigail Díaz es actualmente una estudiante de segundo año que asiste a La Joya Early College. Ella es la hija de Saúl y Patricia Díaz. Le gusta dibujar en su tiempo libre y le gusta cocinar por las mañanas.

# First love

I wished her no harm.
I always wished her the best.

All I ever wanted in the eyes of my princess
Is for her to see me as her prince.
I hope that I am the only one she loves,
But I know I am not.

I watched her grow up,
over the years.

I was there when she cried.
I was there when she laughed.

All I ever wanted from her was her trust
Even when things got rough.
I wanted her to know that I loved her.
From the moment I laid eyes on her
'Till the day I die.

Your first love,

Dad.

-Kenyacelestina Salinas

Kenyacelestina Salinas is 16 years old and is a student at La Joya Early College High School. She is the daughter of Timoteo and Kenia Salinas and sister to Berthaemilia Salinas.

# Primer amor

No le deseé daño.
Siempre le deseé lo mejor.

Todo lo que siempre quise a los ojos de mi princesa
es que yo sea su príncipe azul.
Espero ser el único que ame,
Pero la verdad es que no lo soy.

La vi crecer
Al paso de los años.

Estaba allí cuando ella lloró.
Estaba allí cuando ella se rió.

Todo lo que siempre quise de ella fue su confianza
Incluso cuando las cosas se pusieron difíciles.
Quería que supiera que la amaba.
Desde el momento en que la vi
hasta el día de mi muerte.

Tu primer amor,

Papá.

-*Kenyacelestina Salinas*

Kenyacelestina Salinas is 16 years old and is a student at La Joya Early College High School. She is the daughter of Timoteo and Kenia Salinas and sister to Berthaemilia Salinas.

# Mi Mayor Bendición

La forma en que cuidas todas tus flores de tu jardín,
con ternura y amabilidad.
La forma en que alimentas a las aves,
que casualmente vuelan alrededor.
Es lo mismo cuando das a aquellos,
que no tienen nada que darte a cambio.
La forma en que le dices buenos días al sol,
Incluso si el sol no te lo responde.
Me encanta que tienes un gran corazón.
Me encanta la forma en que estas tan agradecida con,
Dios por otro dia mas.
Incluso cuando tu mundo parece desmoronarse.
 Pero sigues avanzando con la cabeza en alto,
sin dejar que nada ni nadie te quite la alegría que tienes en tu corazón.
Nunca dejaras de ser la mejor madre que da los mejores,
consejos de la vida.
Has pasado por cosas que todavía estoy,
aprendiendo mientras estoy creciendo.
Pero se que estaras a mi lado durante el camino,
y es por eso que te amo.
Eres mi mayor bendición.

*-Janell Garcia*

Janell Garcia was born on May 24th, 2004 and is 15 years old. She is the daughter of Alberto and Juanita Garcia. She is currently a 10th-grader at La Joya Early College High School and a resident of Mission, Texas.

# Recuerdos

En momentos como este,
miro hacia atrás en el pasado.
Pienso en cuando las cosas,
fueron mejores en la vida.

Recuerdos de cuando era solo una niña,
Jugando con mis muñecas.
Sin cuidado en el mundo,
solo viviendo mi vida de cada dia.

Recuerdos de mí creciendo en una adolescente,
soñando con ser un adulto.
Sueños que no se han sido cumplidos,
pero arruinados en el proceso.

Ahora solo pienso en regresar,
regresar a esos recuerdos que me trajeron alegría.
Pero lamentablemente ya es demasiado tarde para volver,
todo lo que puedo hacer ahora es estar agradecida por esos recuerdos.

Esos recuerdos que me hicieron quien soy hoy,
y que me enseñaron lecciones valiosas.
Esos recuerdos que siempre tendré en mi corazón,
por siempre y para siempre.

-*Cynthia Cantú*

Cynthia Cantú nació el 28 de febrero de 2002 y tiene 18 años. Es hija de Javier y Maricela Cantú. Actualmente es estudiante de 12 ° grado en La Joya Early College High School, y es residente de Peñitas, Texas. Su poema se titula: "Recuerdos"

# Memories

In moments like this,
I look back to the past.
I think about when things,
were better in my life.

Memories of when I was just a toddler,
Playing with my dolls.
With no care in the world,
Just living my daily life.

Memories of me growing up as a teenager,
Dreaming of being an adult.
Dreams that were not fulfilled,
But ruined in the process.

Now I think about going back,
and returning to those memories that brought me joy.
But unfortunately it is too late to return,
And all I can do now is be grateful for those memories.

Those memories that made me who I am today,
and that taught me valuable lessons.
Those memories that I will always have in my heart,
forever and always.

-*Cynthia Cantú*

Cynthia Cantú nació el 28 de febrero de 2002 y tiene 18 años. Es hija de Javier y Maricela Cantú. Actualmente es estudiante de 12 ° grado en La Joya Early College High School, y es residente

# Tu forma de ser

Me gusta tu forma de ser
Me encanta tu sonrisa encantadora
Tus ojos castaños brillosos
Tu estilo de vestir me enloquece
Me enloquece cuando haces bromas pequeñas
Y después cuando das un abrazo
Pero…

No me gusta..
No me gusta cómo con esa sonrisa encantadora le sonríes a ella
No me gusta cómo con esos ojos brillosos la miras a ella
No me gusta cómo te vistes para ir a verla a ella
No me gusta cuando le haces bromas pequeñas
Y cuando la abrazas me enloquece,
Me duele que no estés conmigo

*-Perla Conde*


Perla Conde was born on September 3th, 2002 and is 17 years old. She is the daughter of Juan Conde and Candida Hernandez. She is currently a 11th-grade student at La Joya Early College High School. Perla is from Penitas, Texas.

# The way you are

I like the way you are
I love your lovely smile
Your bright brown eyes
Your style of dress drives me crazy
It drives me crazy when you make small jokes
And then when you give a hug
But...

I do not like..
I don't like how with that lovely smile you smile at her
I don't like how you look at her with those bright eyes
I don't like how you dress to go see her
I don't like it when you make small jokes
And when you hug her it drives me crazy,
It hurts that you are not with me

-*Perla Conde*

Perla Conde was born on September 3th, 2002 and is 17 years old. She is the daughter of Juan Conde and Candida Hernandez. She is currently a 11th-grade student at La Joya Early College High School. Perla is from Peñitas, Texas.

# Oh! My Love

There are times when I find myself looking at you with great love
I feel respect for you, I feel fear and curiosity
You always inspire me every step of the way
I secretly peek a little just to see you
You told me that I have an obsession
With the illusion I have of you
I said you were right for not knowing what to say
Now that I'm writing to you,
I tell you that I love you.
that obsession you say I have is not bad
Not at all
It's called admiration
I admire in all that I can
You're a great person
God put you in my life
I see that God is great in me,
In you and in every love of mine.
An inspiration for my life and heart
You always make me scream with emotion.

-Jessica Chavarria


Jessica Chavarria is a junior in La Joya Early College High School and is 16 years of age. She wrote The poem Oh my love which is dedicated to her special someone.

# Oh! Mi Amor

Hay veces cuando me encuentro mirándote con gran cariño
Siento  respeto hacia ti, siento miedo y curiosidad
Siempre me inspiras a cada paso del camino
Secretamente me asomo un poco sólo para verte
Me has dicho que tengo una obsesión
Con la ilusión que tengo de ti
Dije que estabas en lo correcto por no saber qué decir
Ahora que te estoy escribiendo,
Te digo que te amo.
esa obsesión que dices que tengo no es mala
Para nada
Se llama admiración
Admiro en todo lo que puedo
Eres una gran persona
Dios te puso en mi vida
Veo que Dios es grande en mí,
en ti y en cada amor mío.
Una inspiración para mi vida y corazón
Siempre haces que grite de emoción.

-Jessica Chavarria


Jessica Chavarria is a junior in La Joya Early College High School and is 16 years of age. She wrote The poem Oh my love which is dedicated to her special someone.

# Veterans

To those that haven't served
Will never fully be able to understand
The battles and sacrifices you faced
On and off the field.
The sacrifices you were required to do
On and off duty,
And missing out on what's back at home.
The struggles you faced at boot camp to get you to be on the field
The many scars that you are now left with you today.

We recognize everything you did
We see humanity, love, compassion, and pride all through you.
You will always be missed on the field and
To those that didn't get to see tomorrow will always be remembered,
And be honored in our hearts.

Veterans are tough people facing reality,
And what's left of their memory of battle.
You show your toughness by getting through each day
Knowing you have accomplished America's heart.

-Alex Munguia

Alexis Munguia was born on January 7,2004. She is 16 year old and currently attends La Joya Early College High School as a sophomore. She is the daughter of Eliodoro Munguia Jr. and Maria Munguia. Her poem is titled: "Veterans" and is dedicated to her brother.

# Monstrous

A veces no nos sentimos lo mejor de nuestra habilidad
Nos metemos dentro nuestra mente y salen nuestros monstruos que tenemos
Nos dicen cosas que nos hacen triste y nos hacen llorar
Cuando estamos con los que queremos, están detrás de nosotros,
les ponemos sonrisas que no son verdaderas ,para que piensen que estamos bien.
Nuestros monstruos son más ruidosos el la noche porque saben que es cuando estamos solos y no tenemos a nadie para distraernos y tienen toda nuestra atención
Nos dicen cosas que nos llega al corazón y hasta que ya no podemos contenerlo , lloramos hasta que ya no nos salen más lágrimas
 sentimos la necesidad de distraernos con música para liberarnos de nuestra tristeza .Nuestros monstruos también nos hace distanciarnos de los que más amamos.ellos están detrás de nosotros haciendo que dudemos de nosotros mismos y de los que rodean nuestra vida con felicidad .
Nos hacen que no nos amemos a nosotros mismos aunque otros nos los digan, siempre pensamos lo opuesto y cuando nos vemos en el espejo no nos reconocemos. Vemos a alguien que no somos
Vemos a alguien con felicidad que nosotros no podemos obtener . Y esto son nuestros monstruos

-*Diana Perales*

Actualmente, Diana es estudiante de La Joya Early College en el noveno grado. Nació el 23 de octubre de 2004 en Orlando, Florida, pero se crió en Texas.

# Atrapada

Lo mas que trate de olvidarte
No creo que podre
Tu estas conmigo a cada instante
Estas siempre en mi mente

¿El amor te hace sentir todo esto?
Sentir que corres en la nubes
Y estar sumergida a lo más hondo de la tierra
Al mismo tiempo

Todo me hace recordarte
Miro el cielo y pienso en tus ojos
Los que vi llorar mientras decías adiós
Por última vez

Me pregunto si a veces piensas en mí como yo a ti
Si miras algo que te recuerde a mi
A nosotras
Todo está en el pasado ahora

Tu por tu lado y yo por el mío
Aunque estemos lejos de una a la otra
Siempre habrá un espacio para ti en este corazón frágil que poco a poco se recupera de tu pérdida

-Nayra I. Estrada

Nayra I. Estrada is a senior at La Joya Early College High School. She is 17 years old and is a resident of Sullivan City, Texas.

# A Love Story

In my house on my dresser in a pot, there's a cactus.
He's small and has cute stingers all around.
Next to the window in the sill he never lacks, thus,
He's always smiling in the sunlight, never frowns.

Until one fateful day, a flower stole his spot.
I rushed quick to fill a vase, lest it wilt.
I set it on the sill next to my cactus,
And the look on his poor face, it could have killed.

They say brimstone is the worst of all hell's tortures,
But cacti are the exception to the rule,
His pointers prickled as he planned his plot,
To spurn him, this he swore, this I would rue.

Come nightfall, as I slept, the time was nigh,
His thirst for just revenge finally slaked,
As I slept, atop my night clock, there he lies,
Bristles primed, the trap is set, he lies in wait.

So come sunrise, rising with the crack of dawn,
My alarm clock blared and blasted to no end,
I threw my hand upon the clock fast as I yawned,
And found, to my surprise, my prickly friend.

The end.

-Sebastian Sy

Sebastian Sy, A Love Story, A high school student who just can't get enough of putting words on a page at ungodly hours late at night. He likes tea over coffee, dogs over cats, and believes everyone deserves a voice except for people who put pineapple on pizza.

# The Botany of Dreams

If our dreams could touch the sky
Do you think they would? Like the stem of a
Sunflower, petals grasping rays of sun
Too thin, shards of simultaneous
Despair and acquisition glistening, luring,
Cutting into delicate yellow flesh, the
Fruit of the flower split, and then
They hover, trickle softly to the ground,
Browning, burning, sliced by the sunshine's
fervent, feigned promises- Do our
Dreams grow towards the sun? Do they tilt to the
Great star's bidding? Do their leaves uplift, overturn,
Open to summer's exhausting heat of opportunity?

Or do they grow, like
Branches on a tree? Heavy, steady, its
Trunk moaning, cracking with each passing storm,
Its roots delving deep into rich black soil of the mind, the
Granulated expanse of thought and mineral, granules of
Nutrients plumping root hairs with Hope- Do our
Branches extend to the ends of the Earth? Do they shade the grass
Below us, blossoming for itself a supple fruit? Do its roots become
Entangled while chasing their own dreams?

But maybe they'd rot, as all plants do-
Left to be composted and buried to
Nourish, supplement the roots and being of another. The
Bark of our branches will rot with age and drought,
The golden petals of our sunflower will wilt in
Darkness and winter.

-Amanda Rose Garcia

Amanda Garcia is a senior at the Science Academy of South Texas. Just recently delving into the art of poetry, she began writing last year as an outlet of unbounded self-expression.

# Extraño

Extraño esos bellos momentos de mi niñez
Siempre andaba con mi mami y papi
Agarrada de sus manos con una sonrisa oreja a oreja

Esos largos viajes por carretera
Cantando nuestros canciones favoritas
Eran mi favorito

Son lo que mas adoro

Aunque se que un dia me ire de casa
quisiera poder quedarme en sus brazos para siempre

-*Analee Castillo*

La Joya Early College High School. Es hija de Arnoldo y Liliana Castillo.

# Innocencia

El niño corriendo en el terreno de su casa
jugando fútbol con sus hermanas
no sabiendo nada del mundo cruel
su corazón lleno de amor y felicidad

El niño con el corazón de oro
empatía para todos humanos y animales
su alma tan pura e inocente
sin corrupción del mundo fuera de la cerca de su mundo
Su mundo tan pequeño e inocente

Su mundo destruido por el coraje de los monstruos afuera
 Su inocencia rompida de su corazón
La herida que dejó en su alma sangrò y sangrò
Sangrò hasta que todo de su alma
Quedó en el piso agotado de toda pura

Todo lo que quedó del niño fue coraje, dolor y venganza
Todo lo bueno que él antes conoció en su mundo inocente
Se ha ido de su mente y alma para siempre
Y su inocencia corrupta como todos los demás

-Christian Castaneda

Christian Castaneda es el hijo de la familia aldape. El tiene una hermana y es el único hombre de su familia.

# Dad

I couldn't ask you for anymore.
Everytime i'm in a tough situation
You're the first one that's there.
No other Father-Son relationship is able to compare.
All our fishing trips are filled with joy
That no experience can top it, not even a new toy.
You taught me everything from riding a bike
Even to fix a leaky pipe.
You showed me the good from the bad
And teaching me how to understand.
You've given me everything I've asked for
And you've opened so many doors.
I want to explore what they call Earth with you
Since the day of my own birth.
Dad I couldn't love you anymore.

-*Noe Bazan*

Noe Bazan Jr was born April 23, 2005. He is the son of Noe Bazan and Leticia Valdez. He is currently a 9th-grade student at La Joya Early College and a resident of Mission, Texas. His poem is titled: Dad.

# Padre

No puedo preguntarte por nada más.
Cada vez que estoy en una situacion difícil
Tu eres el primero que está allí.
Ningún otra Padre-Hijo relación puede comparar.
Todos nuestros viajes de pescar estan llenas de alegría.
Que no experiencia puede superar, ningún juguete nuevo.
Me enseñaste todo a montar en bicicleta
A componer una pipa agujereada.
Me enseñaste lo bueno a lo malo
Y me enseñaste cómo comprender.
Me has dado todo lo que he pedido
Y has abierto muchas puertas para mi.
Quiero explorar todo que se llama el Mundo con tigo
Desde el dia que nacie.
Padre no puedo amarte más.

*-Noe Bazan*

Noe Bazan Jr was born April 23, 2005. He is the son of Noe Bazan and Leticia Valdez. He is currently a 9th-grade student at La Joya Early College and a resident of Mission, Texas. His poem is titled: Dad.

# Blank

We sit in class
All day long
Listening to them
The teachers
Talk Talk Talk

We sit, and we listen
All day long
They want us to write
The teachers
Write Write Write

We sit, and we listen, and we write
All day long
They expect us to be quiet
The teachers
Quiet Quiet Quiet

We sit, and we listen, we write and be quiet
All day long
They expect us to be nice
The teachers
Nice Nice Nice

But not everyone is
Not everything looks perfect

The repetition of everyday
Hour
Rep Repiti Repetition

We sit there
All day long
Our minds go blank
The stress
Blank Blank Blank

*-Liora Vela*

Liora Vela is currently a freshman at La Joya Early College, still trying to go through high school. In "Blank" describing how it feels to deal with teachers at school.

# Blanco

Nosotros nos sentamos en clase
Todo el dia
Escuchándolos
Los maestros
Hablar Hablar Hablar

Nos sentamos y escuchamos
Toda el dia
Ellos quieren que escribamos
Los maestros
Escribir Escribir Escribir

Nos sentamos y escuchamos y escribimos
Todo el dia
Esperan que estemos callados
Los maestros
Silencio Silencio Silencio

Nos sentamos y escuchamos, escribimos y callamos
Todo el dia
Quieren que nosotros somos agradables
Los maestros
Agradable Agradable Agradable

Pero no todos son
No todo se ve perfecto

La repetición de lo cotidiano
Hora
Rep Repeti Repetición

Nosotros nos sentamos ahí
Todo el dia
Nuestras mentes se quedan en blanco
Del estrés
Blanco Blanco Blanco

*-Liora Vela*

Liora Vela is currently a freshman at La Joya Early College, still trying to go through high school. In "Blank" describing how it feels to deal with teachers at school.

# El caballo de mis sueños

Cuando primero lo vi supe que sería mío
Su color era un negro oscuro
Su cabello era largo y brilloso
Su paso era elegante
Su baile era incomparable
Ningún otro caballo se comparaba con el Cuervo
Él era uno en un millón
Él había viajado mucho
 para llegar a mis manos
Recorrió todo México
Y por donde él estaba era apreciado
Por todos que lo miraban
Pasó por muchas playas mexicanas
Por montañas
Y por mi corazón
Este era  mi caballo
El Cuervo

-*Jesus Jimenez*

Jesus Jimenez was born on September 17,2003.He is 16 years old. He is the son of Manuel Jimenez and Irma Jimenez. He is currently a 10th grader attending La Joya early college.

# The horse of my dreams

When I first saw him,
I knew he would be mine
His color was a dark black
His hair was long and shiny
His step was elegant
His dance was incomparable
No other horse was compared to the him
He was one in a million
He had traveled far and wide
 to reach me
He toured all of Mexico
And where he would be
 he was appreciated
For all that looked at him
He passed through many
Mexican beaches, mountains
And through my heart
This was my horse
The Raven

-Jesus Jimenez

Jesus Jimenez was born on September 17,2003. He is 16 years old. He is the son of Manuel Jimenez and Irma Jimenez. He is currently a 10th grader attending La Joya early college.

# Dilemas

Cuántas vueltas da la vida
A veces abajo y otras arriba
Un día estás
Y al otro ya no más

Que incrédulo es pensar
Que el tiempo puede perdonar
Los días pasan y pasan
Pero el recordar me atrasa
Tanta cosa me rebasa

Lo que es y lo que puede ser
No hay manera de saber
Aún así me atormenta
Y en la noche me mantiene despierta.

-Miranda Jimenez

Miranda Jiménez is an eleventh grader at la Joya Early College. She's a resident of Mission, Texas.

# Hermanito

Recuerdo esos momentos solitarios
Sin nadie con quién jugar a diario
Después de tanto aburrimiento
Llegó una noticia a cambiar el cuento
Cada día que pasaba
Sólo en felicidad pensaba
Recuerdo el día en que llegaste
Mi vida cambiaste
Han pasado doce años y siempre te brindaré apoyo
Hermanito, eres el complemento de mi vida
Contigo nunca me daré por vencida

*-Yanelly Licea*

Yanelly Licea es una estudiante en La Joya Early College High school. Ella tiene 17 años de edad.

# Cosmetics ≠ Society

Many times, I have been on the situation where people tell me:
"Why do you wear so much makeup" "You're prettier without makeup"
"You don't look like yourself with makeup"
Well obviously. I don't spend my money on makeup to look the same.
OH and don't think I do my makeup to impress boys.
OBVIOUSLY NOT.
I do this because it's what I truly enjoy.
It all started when I was 12 years old.
My cousin didn't have someone that would allow him to do their makeup.
So I stepped in.
One day, I decided to ask what was the thing that had like a million colors.
"Es una paleta"
"Ohhh a lollipop" -I said
Laughing he told me that it was an eyeshadow palette.
As I grew older, I bought my own palette. I remember I bought it at Burlington.
I started watching Youtube videos about makeup.
I was very inspired by James Charles.
I decided to buy his palette in collaboration with Morphe.
I played with it day and night.
I unleashed my inner artist.
Every time I go to the makeup store

I want to buy eyeshadow palettes
But my mother thinks I have more than enough palettes
Apparently 23 palettes are a lot for her.
My parents have never told me not to wear makeup.
But society is always judging us for the things we do and for the things we don't do.
So honestly if you think my eyelashes are too big and that they will be blown away by the air,
I honestly don't care.
If you think my lips are too red,
Come here I have a red shade that will match your attitude perfectly.

-*Grecia Solis*

Grecia Solis was born on December 10, 2004. Her parents are Francisco Solis and Ismelda Solis. She really enjoys makeup. In her free time she likes to do her makeup. Her poem is titled: Cosmetics ≠ Society.

# El Amor es Hermoso

Amor
Es algo que todos anhelamos
Un sentimiento que es inexplicable
Una sensación que queremos ricos o pobres.

Amor
Todos lo necesitamos
Para sobrevivir,
Para vivir.

Amor
Si no la tenemos,
Nos volvemos locos,
Nos sentimos solos.

Amor
Es un escape,
Un escape del mundo,
Si estuviéramos libres de todo

Amor
Es inexplicable,
Un escape,
El amor es hermoso.

-Natalie Viveros

Natalie Viveros nació en Virginia y actualmente reside en Peñitas, TX, donde es estudiante de noveno grado en La Joya Early College High School.

# Love is Beautiful

Love
Something we all long for
A feeling that is unexplainable
A sensation we want either rich or poor

Love
We all need it
To survive,
To live.

Love if we don't have it,
We go insane
We feel lonely

Love
Is an escape.
An escape from the world,
As if we're free from everything.

Love
Is unexplainable,
An escape.
Love is beautiful.

-*Natalie Viveros*

Natalie Viveros was born in Virginia and currently resides in Peñitas, TX where she is a 9th grader at La Joya Early College High School

# Anger

Anger
It's a feeling of anger
An instinct that we all have
An angry mother knows:
The Anger

Anger
It's a burning feeling
It's a spark that ignites
A fiery call that burns everything
Around it

Anger
It's a conflict that melts the ice
Destroy peace in our hearts
It's not the warm flame in our hearts
but it is the fiery flame that burns are
Hearts

Anger
It's the devil inside us.
Kill the angel in us and
We are corrupted by it
And it makes us do the unthinkable

-Bryan Beltran

Bryan Beltran is a 15 years old boy that studies at the La Joya Early College High School. His poem is inspired by the feeling of being angry.

# Una vez más

Una vez más es todo lo que pido
Solo para ver tu hermosa sonrisa
Para sentir tus cálidos abrazos
Para escuchar tu maravillosa risa
Sólo una vez más

Solo una vez más para abrazarte
Para sentir tu corazón latir junto al mío
Para sentirse seguro y amado en tus brazos
Para escuchar tus maravillosos consejos
Sólo una vez más

Eso es todo lo que pido una vez más
Si pudiera hacer algo para verte, lo haría
Para ver tus hermosos ojos
Para sentir tus manos suaves
Sólo una vez más…

*-Jewelisa Veloz*

Jewelisa Veloz nació el 10 de febrero de 2005, sus padres son Irma Veloz y Manuel Veloz. Ella es una estudiante de noveno grado en La Joya Early College High School, y es residente de la ciudad de La Joya.

# One more time

One more time is all I ask for
Just to see your beautiful smile
To feel your warm hugs
To hear your wonderful laugh
Just one more time

Just one more time to hold you
To feel your heartbeat next to mine
To feel safe and loved in your arms
To hear your wonderful advice
Just one more time

That's all I ask for one more time
If i could do anything to see you i would
To see your beautiful eyes
To feel your soft hands
Just one more time...

-Jewelisa Veloz


Jewelisa Veloz was born February 10th 2005 her parents are Irma Veloz and Manuel Veloz.she is a 9th grader at La Joya Early College High School ,and she is a resident of the city of La Joya, TX.

# Felicidad

Felicidad es un sentimiento hermoso.
No sabemos como explicarlo,
pero sonreímos
y tambien brincamos.

Felicidad es algo que no puedes comprar,
en cualquier momento la puedes tomar.
Solo tienes que decidir,
que es la mejor opción para ti.

La felicidad va y viene
Y no se queda siempre con el que la obtiene.
La felicidad es algo que todos quieren,
Pero sabemos que se fue cuando las risas no suenen.

Si algun dia sientes felicidad,
Apreciala sin parar.
Úsala en cualquier momento,
No importa si es en algo tonto.

*-Jazive Martinez-Ramirez*

Jazive Martinez-Ramirez es una estudiante de noveno grado en La Joya Early College High School. Jazibe es la hija de Ramiro A. Martinez y Maria Ramirez. Jazibe es residente de los Ebanos, Texas.

# Happiness

Happiness is a beautiful feeling.
We don't know how to explain it,
but we smile
And we also jump.

Happiness is something you can't buy,
at any time you can take it.
You just have to decide,
If it is the best option for you.

Happiness comes and goes
And it doesn't always stay with the one who gets it.
Happiness is something everyone wants,
But we know it left when the laughter is gone.

If one day you feel happiness,
Appreciate it without stopping.
Use it anytime,
It doesn't matter if it's something silly.

-*Jazive Martinez-Ramirez*

Jazive Martinez-Ramirez is currently a 9th grade student of La Joya Early College High School. Jazibe is the daughter of Ramiro A. Martinez and Maria Ramirez. Jazibe is a resident of Los Ebanos, Texas.

# Creciendo

Todos en un momento tienen miedo de crecer
¿Por qué tenemos miedo de envejecer?
Envejecer significa que todos a tu alrededor
Envejecen y mueren

A medida que pasa el tiempo,
crecerás alejado de gente
Las personas a tu alrededor tendrán familia
Y se olvidaran de ti
Tendras una familia propia
Y también te olvidarás de la gente

Envejecer significa muchas cosas malas
Pero también puede significar cosas buenas
Como una familia, una casa, un trabajo que disfrutas
Todos van a envejecer un día
Y solo debemos sacar lo mejor de nuestra juventud

-*Mayeli Guzman*

Mayeli Guzman es una estudiante de noveno grado en La Joya Early College High School. Mayeli es residente en Palmview, Texas y tiene 14 años.

# Dam

The words have stopped flowing from within my head
Yet all my fingertips crave is for it to resume again
For the feelings to manifest as letters
And stories as the words driven from the mind's gutters
Whereupon lives are born from sentences
And cities of words form beautiful spectacles

Yet the dam that I had built before
To hold back the words that seemed to escape from my every pore
Seems to serve no purpose,
Becoming an eye-sore forming sores in the recently wordless
My mind, now a desert where once a beautiful ocean breathed life into my lungs
And the seafloor had been plagued with cities of coral and sponge
But it's all gone now and all that remains are ruins of necrosis and rot
The Cities lie crumbled and decrepit on the desert floor of lost thoughts

The dam serves no purpose.
A monument standing to remind me of the words that flowed in earnest
A monument to the momentous, momentary monopoly on the word-tsunamis

A monstrous memento that monody's the life of the words that lived as the ocean's stories

A highrise paperweight sits on the deserted desk in my room,
And has become an obsolescent tool

-*Efrain Ibarra*

Efrain Ibarra is a fifteen year old boy that was born in South Texas. He's had his fair share of emotional problems and personal situations and circumstances, yet, despite feeling otherwise untalented, he's always had a passion for writing. Soon, he learned to command words into art.

# Hourglasses Tick

Time moves slow
Moving in sync with a rowers row
Seconds cumulate
At a steady rate
Minutes congregate
Not a second too late
Hours start to form
Locked in a glass case brewing a sandstorm
With each second that comes to pass
The grains of sand pile in mass
Caged in a shell of their fired brethren
A horrid sight that's transparent
Ironic to be locked in a timetracker
For all of time and no later.
There's no such thing as "brief"
When using the hourglass's motif
Can't you hear them falling?
Their yelling and thudding?
If sand makes noise when it lands,
Isn't there a tick or tock from falling sand?
As does a clock, the hourglass ticks
Building the day out of its sandy bricks
Seconds are borrowed
But each make up every long hour
Time moves slow
It ebbs and flows

Eroding moments in time
Following an internal rhyme
Tick, tick, tick
Tick, tock, tick

-*Efrain Ibarra*

Efrain Ibarra is a fifteen year old boy that was born in South Texas. He's had his fair share of emotional problems and personal situations and circumstances, yet, despite feeling otherwise untalented, he's always had a passion for writing. Soon, he learned to command words into art.

# If you gave a person immortality and a myriad of things, what would they do?

Give me a pair scissors and I'll cut in a heartfelt way
Give me a knife and I'll cut straightaway
Give me a pen and I'll write a screenplay
Give me a pencil and I'll draw a gloomy day
Give me an eraser and I'll will it all away
For I want only something to say

Give me Immortality and I'll wish to die
Give me a sad moment and I'll wish to cry
Give me a beautiful day and I'll only sigh
Give me something to hate and I'll wish it goodbye
Give me memories and I'll wonder where it went awry
For I want only to see life through another's eye

Give me a sword and I'll fight
Give me an enemy and I'll smite
Give me an army and I'll be traveling by first light
Give me a gun and I'll find a line of sight
Give me a loss and I'll disappear overnight
For I live only in fright

Give me someone to love and I'll have a friend
Give me someone who loves me and I won't comprehend
Give me a long distance away and I'll wait for the weekend

Give me a hater and I'll wait for the next friend
Give me a life and I'll pretend
For I am just a horrible person
For I am a Pen,
Give me blood.
Forgive my Ink.

*-Efrain Ibarra*

Efrain Ibarra is a fifteen year old boy that was born in South Texas. He's had his fair share of emotional problems and personal situations and circumstances, yet, despite feeling otherwise untalented, he's always had a passion for writing. Soon, he learned to command words into art.

# Fue un error

Fue un error conocerte y contarte todo de mí,
Nuestra amistad era única
Pero un grande error causó que nuestra amistad se derrumbara.

Yo pensando que tu nunca me harías mal,
Pero me estás pagando a una manera que no merezco.

Fue un error confiar en ti
Tu sonrisa y forma de ser me daba alegría
Pero al verte en estos momentos me da coraje.

El momento en donde me di cuenta que me estás pagando de esa manera,
Yo no sabía cómo reaccionar pero al momento no pude detener mis lágrimas.

Fui una inútil por creer en ti,
Por tus acciones qué estás haciendo no estás haciendo bien para ninguno de los dos.
Pero pues ya tomaste acción y lamentablemente no hay manera de regresar al tiempo para no cometer nuestro error.

Fue un error dedicarte tanto de mi tiempo para que todo se terminara
Fuimos un error,

Pero lo de nosotros está en el pasado.

-*Desaree Guajardo*

Desaree Guajardo is a 10th grader at La Joya Early College. She is the daughter of Efraín Guajardo and Claudia Mercado.

# It was a mistake

It was a mistake to meet you and tell you all about me,
Our friendship was unique
But a big mistake caused our friendship to collapse.

Me thinking that you would never hurt me
But you are paying me in a way that I don't deserve.

It was a mistake to trust you
Your smile and way of being gave me joy
But seeing you right now gives me anger.

The moment I realized that you're paying me that way,
I didn't know how to react but at the moment I couldn't stop my tears.

I was dumb for believing in you,
For your actions you are not doing well for either of us.
But then you already took action and unfortunately there is no way to return to time to not make our mistake.

It was a mistake to dedicate so much of my time for everything to end
We were a mistake,
But ours is in the past.

-Desaree Guajardo

Desaree Guajardo is a 10th grader at La Joya Early College. She is the daughter of Efraín Guajardo and Claudia Mercado.

# Fácil

Fácil crees que soy
Crees que con bromas,
sonrisas y halagos llegarás a mi corazón
El pasado hizo a la persona
Desconfío de un hombre sin tener una razón
Sé quien soy y a dónde voy
Un hombre podrá difamarme
por ser indomable e incansable
Pero él nunca podrá definirme
Y por ser mujer no me rendiré tan fácil ante tus pies
Y un "te amo" ilusiona y pero nunca perdona

-Jacquelyn Hernandez

Jacquelyn Hernandez is 18 years old. She currently attends La Joya Early College High School.

www.ingramcontent.com/pod-product-compliance
Lightning Source LLC
Chambersburg PA
CBHW020351080526
44584CB00014B/975